T0206872

Asylums, Treatment Centers and Genetic Jails

ASYLUMS, TREATMENT CENTERS AND GENETIC JAILS

A HISTORY OF MINNESOTA STATE HOSPITALS

MICHAEL A. RESMAN, MA, OTR (RETIRED)

NORTH STAR PRESS OF ST. CLOUD, INC.

Saint Cloud, Minnesota

Copyright © 2013 Michael A. Resman

Cover image courtesy of the Minnesota Historical Society
Cover image: Fergus Falls State Hospital ca 1900

ISBN: 978-0-87839-618-4

All rights reserved.

Patients names have been omitted throughout the book, as have the names of all but public figures. The intent is not to castigate former staff, but to provide an understanding of the milieu in the medical community and Minnesota that led to what happened in state hospitals.

Unless otherwise noted, all primary source materials are from the library at the Minnesota History Center.

Printed in the United States of America

Published by
North Star Press of St. Cloud, Inc.
St. Cloud, Minnesota
www.northstarpress.com

TABLE OF CONTENTS

FOREWORD

S TATE HOSPITALS HOUSED THOUSANDS of patients. When families had concerns, they often wrote to the head office in St. Paul. The following letter was sent to Dr. Royal Gray, the chief of the State Mental Health Unit in the 1950s.

St. Paul, MN

Gentlemen:—

I am writing you concerning the St. Peter State Hospital.

My father, (_____), became a patient there the latter part of last January. When we took him there we were under the impression that he would be given treatment for a mental illness. We do not find that anything is being done except to confine him in much the same manner as is used for criminals.

We were given the name of his physician, but have never been able to locate the elusive doctor. Everywhere we are confronted with the same impersonal disinterest. The superintendent gave us the reassurance that he was not causing any trouble—which was not what we were concerned about. We want to know what is being done for him if anything, besides having a frail, little old man of nearly seventy years scrubbing floors. Each time we visit he looks more frail, but nothing at all is being done.

I would greatly appreciate any advice you can give me.

Sincerely,

Mrs. (_____)[1]

In contrast to the preceding letter is a note in the Rochester record from 1948:

> _____ *'s husband had permission to take his wife for a ride. In the evening he called and stated they were in Minneapolis and could not make it back, but that he would bring her back the next day. The Dr. informed him that he must have her back in the hospital that next day. He has not returned her to date. Therefore, we are carrying her on our records as escaped.*[2]

I am an amateur historian, and must admit I'm biased toward being an advocate for people with mental disabilities. At times, I was moved to tears by what I found when researching asylums and mental hospitals in Minnesota. I also cheered upon uncovering an all too infrequent triumph. There are stories that could be written and facts to dig out for years to come. I hope others do so.

---

1. Public Welfare Department, the correspondence of Dr. Royal Gray, MD, Chief, Mental Health Unit
2. Rochester State Hospital, movement of population records

INTRODUCTION

MINNESOTA'S STATE HOSPITALS WERE first conceived as asylums—places of refuge where people who behaved oddly could be cared for. Unlike the ostracism, exploitation, neglect or suffering they may have experienced in their home communities, they would be sheltered and safe.

Little treatment was available for most of the first one hundred years. Sedatives and a variety of interventions were attempted on a limited basis with the aim of calming patients.

Beginning in the early 1900s, state hospitals were seen as a means to prevent defective people from reproducing. The number of patients quickly grew, outpacing resources for the next fifty years. Overcrowding led to neglect and resulted in patient regression. Restraints came into wide usage as small numbers of staff struggled to maintain control over hospital wards that could become chaotic and dangerous.

In the 1950s, psychiatry turned to innovative treatments in an attempt to improve the functioning of many patients. Many interventions that calmed patients were introduced, including insulin, shock treatments and lobotomies. By the 1960s, many of these crude—and damaging—treatments were abandoned in favor of medications.

The modern era of psychiatry resulted in widespread discharges from state hospitals, first to nursing homes and later into the community. Several Minnesota state hospitals were converted to prisons. Populations in the others gradually declined, with a few buildings still in use for treatment programs.

Asylums, Treatment Centers and Genetic Jails

CHAPTER ONE
CONSTRUCTION CHRONOLOGY

ONE OF THE FIRST ISSUES THE NEWLY FORMED Minnesota state government addressed was what to do with people who drank too much or acted strangely. The first meeting of the territorial legislature gave judges custody of idiots, lunatics, and habitual drunks who could not manage their own property.[1]

As county governments organized in Minnesota, lunatic persons were often placed in almshouses and poor farms if they were quiet and cooperative. Those who were disruptive were jailed.[2]

A limited number of patients were placed in the Iowa hospital for the insane beginning in 1862. Governor Alexander Ramsey agreed to pay $4.74 per week for each patient. They were transported by steamboat to Mt. Pleasant, Iowa, along with a year's worth of clothing.

The Institute for the Deaf, Dumb, and Blind opened in Faribault in 1863 as a boarding school. In 1874, buildings were constructed so the deaf school could function separately from the blind school. For eight years, beginning in 1879, an experimental school for the feeble-minded was part of the organization but then split off. The blind and deaf schools were administered in St Paul by the same department that oversaw state hospitals until 1977, when they came under the Department of Education. They were considered schools and not hospitals, so their history is not covered in this book.

ST. PETER

BY 1866, THE IOWA HOSPITAL FOR THE INSANE was nearly full, and Minnesota was informed that all patients would be returned as soon as possible.[3]

While the first law regarding the insane was aimed primarily at defining property rights, fifteen years later a commitment law was passed. The legislature approved the establishment of a hospital for the insane and stipulated that the community selected had to donate at least twenty acres for the site. Competition between communities was fierce.[4]

One of the possibilities considered was a newly constructed building in St. Anthony, intended for the University of Minnesota. Regent John Pillsbury opposed the idea, arguing that the new institution of higher learning shouldn't be converted into an insane asylum.

St. Peter beat out Red Wing by formally offering a 210-acre farm and an empty hotel to serve as a temporary hospital. A local group raised $7,000 to buy the farm and renovations began on the former hotel, finishing in December 1866. Two of the first patients were transferred from jail in St. Paul. One was a man who had been incarcerated for three years, the second a women who'd spent ten months in jail and arrived "perfectly covered with lice."[5]

Money was authorized for the construction of a permanent hospital the following year. A quarry on the site provided stone, and a million bricks were made on the hospital farm. The building was completed in sections, with patients gradually moving in between 1870 and 1875.

One night in November 1880, a fire started in the basement of the men's wing and quickly spread up three floors to emerge from the roof. Firefighting efforts were hampered when only a few hoses in the building's hall-

Minnesota Hospital for the Insane ca. 1867, courtesy Minnesota Historical Society. The community of St. Peter won out over other communities vying to be the site of the first state hospital. Pictured here, an old hotel located downtown was donated for temporary use, along with an outlying farm where the permanent hospital would be built.

ways could be reached because of thick smoke. A rubber hose was unreeled but had been stored flattened for so long that water wouldn't flow through it. A woman bystander and later a patient climbed ladders with axes to chop open barred windows in the upper floors to rescue several patients.[6]

Women patients were led downtown to the Nicollet House and Court House and provided with hot beverages. Because their section of the building didn't burn, they were later able to return to the hospital. About a hundred male patients wandered off in the confusion that night and were brought back by area farmers.

Twenty-four patients died and a number of hospital staff were injured. A patient working in food service was found to have started the fire because he entertained a grudge.

Governor Pillsbury and the president of the hospital board of trustees visited the hospital the next day. It was decided to quickly install a heating system in a building being constructed at Rochester and to transfer some patients there. The chapel and some offices at the St. Peter hospital were used to house patients, and Governor Pillsbury offered to provide $35,000 of his own money to repair two sections of the building until the legislature could meet.[7]

ROCHESTER

As St. Peter was filling with mentally disturbed patients, habitual drunkards continued to be a burden to counties. Responding to a growing belief that alcoholism should be treated, the State Medical Society pushed for authorization of a new hospital. Even before the building at St. Peter was completed, the legislature passed a bill taxing all liquor dealers ten dollars to raise funds for an inebriate asylum.[8]

The tax was unpopular but was upheld by the Minnesota Supreme Court.

A large farm on the outskirts of Rochester was purchased, and construction began in 1877. A year later, the liquor tax was repealed. St. Peter was being criticized for being overcrowded, so the Rochester hospital was designated as the second hospital for the insane and would include an alcoholism treatment program. It opened in January 1879.[9]

State Asylum for the Insane, Rochester ca. 1904, courtesy Minnesota Historical Society. Shown here after thirty years of construction, the original hospital consisted of wing after wing of interconnected buildings.

Construction of additional buildings had to be rushed late the next year to accommodate patients displaced by the fire at St. Peter.

The hospital land included a sandstone bluff. Beginning in 1882, patients dug a 200-foot circular tunnel to be used as a root cellar. Wagons could be pulled into one end, off-load food into storage bins cut into the sides of the cellar, and exit the other end of the tunnel. The bluff was next to the hospital cemetery, and another tunnel was dug to store bodies during the winter.[10]

The bluff later became an economic boon to the hospital when the back side was used as a quarry.

FARIBAULT

THE SCHOOLS FOR DEAF AND BLIND CHILDREN were directed to open an experimental department for feeble-minded children in 1879. Fifteen children were transferred from Rochester and St. Peter state hospitals to the new School for Idiots and Imbeciles.

The first biennial report of the School for Imbeciles reported that all of the twenty-five pupils made progress. All learned " . . . valuable lessons of decency, order, and cleanliness." Training the special senses and physical education formed the foundation of the educational process because "it is the only way to arouse the dormant minds of such as these." In mustering support for the work of the school, the superintendent stated that, "... it is the duty of this state to provide for the training of this unfortunate class, which, if left to itself, rapidly degenerates and becomes, in many instances, dangerous to a degree far beyond that possible to those afflicted with the milder forms of insanity." He claimed that defectives were "largely recruited" from the tide of immigrants.[11]

The three functions of the institution were:

> 1. The education of the high-grade pupil by properly adapted school, shop and farm occupations, in preparation for life outside the institution under favorable conditions. 2. To tenderly, humanely and economically care for the very helpless child whose presence in the home entails a burden too heavy and exacting for the family to bear. 3. To provide the intermediate grade, incapable of adaptation in the outside world, useful employment, congenial companionship and a good home.[12]

Main Building, School for Feeble-minded ca. 1905, courtesy Minnesota Historical Society. Construction of facilities to house people with developmental disabilities would continue at this and other sites—and continues today, if small private groups homes are considered.

Construction would continue to expand the facilities on the extensive grounds for the next seventy-five years.

Fergus Falls

Six years after Rochester opened as the second hospital for the insane, the increasing number of patients led the legislature to approve the creation of a third hospital, to be located at Fergus Falls. Construction didn't begin until two years later, on what would become one of the largest buildings ever constructed by the state. Towering a full four stories plus a steep attic, it eventually sprawled for what would be two city blocks.

A tour of the new hospital revealed that the rooms were in readiness with the very best all-wool mattresses and down pillows. Just five days before patients were due to arrive, it was discovered that the basement was too small to accommodate the laundry machines, boilers and pumps, so a temporary brick addition was added.[13]

The local paper announced that eighty lunatics had arrived by special train from St. Peter on July 30, 1890. The patients were all male and described as the quieter and mild type who would be employed at the asylum.[14]

Postcard, Fergus Falls State Hospital ca. 1915, courtesy Minnesota Historical Society. The hospital towered over the prairie in northwest Minnesota.

Fergus Falls State Hospital ca. 1900, courtesy Minnesota Historical Society. This photo shows some of the architectual flourishes included in the design.

GILLETTE

RESPONDING TO THE NEEDS OF CHILDREN with physical disabilities, the University of Minnesota was given authority, in 1897, to establish a Minnesota Institute for Crippled and Indigent Children. It first opened as a single ward in the City and County Hospital in St. Paul. The university regents named Dr. Gillette as chief surgeon and medical school staff donated their services. The state provided braces and surgical appliances.

The hospital was created to serve indigent children from the ages of two to sixteen living in the state for at least a year who were crippled, deformed, or were suffering from a disease through which they were likely to become crippled or deformed. Patients with conditions considered incurable were not admitted. During the first year, exclusions included infantile paralysis and progressive muscular atrophy.

The most common condition seen in the hospital during its first year derived from orthopedic tuberculosis diseases of the spine, hip, knee, and ankle. Congenital club feet and dislocated hips were surgically addressed. Children with cerebral palsy, burn contractures, and scoliosis were also treated.

The Board of Regents had been given the task of inaugurating the hospital for two years by the legislature. At the end of that time, they said that the work was "entirely foreign to the duties of the Board of Regents" and asked that the legislature assign the task to another agency.[15]

As the number of patients grew, funds were solicited from citizens and the Business League and Commercial Club of St. Paul to purchase land near Phalen Park. The Minnesota State Hospital for Indigent, Crippled and Deformed Children opened in 1911. Dr. Gillette died ten years later, and the name was changed to the Gillette State Hospital for Crippled Children.

Anoka and Hastings

It had become clear in operating state hospitals for twenty years that many insane patients didn't improve. It was decided to separate the chronic patients from those who might improve and return home. This would require the construction of an additional hospital to act as an asylum—providing care but few treatment efforts.

A commission was appointed to select a new site. It visited Anoka in the fall of 1895, but voted four to three to select the town of Hastings. Bowing to pressure to locate a hospital in the northern part of the state, the commission held another vote a week later and Anoka won.

Hastings went to court to try to prevent the state from buying a site on the outskirts of Anoka for $15,000. The court decided in Anoka's favor in April, ruling that the commission had acted within its responsibilities. Hastings appealed the decision to the State Supreme Court, seeking a permanent injunction. The Supreme Court sustained the lower court decision. Finally, both towns turned to the legislature with a plan to build two hospitals.

The 1899 legislature authorized the creation of the first state asylum at Anoka, and a second asylum at Hastings. Ground was broken at the Anoka site in June 1899. The first patients were admitted in March 1900. A hundred patients who were considered incurable were transferred from St. Peter in special train cars, accompanied by nine nurses and a doctor.[16]

Hastings opened a year later, with 112 patients transferred from Rochester. After being open only a year, an inspection filed by the Board of

Visitors in 1901 cited a number of complaints. These included: a water supply impregnated with iron and acid, mildewed tunnels, roaches in the kitchen and women's cottage, uninsulated steam pipes, patients left unattended, gasoline stoves in use in the laundry, dirty beds, dirty dishes, and patients harshly spoken to.[17]

AH-GWAH-CHING

AT THE TURN OF THE TWENTIETH CENTURY, legislative attention turned its focus away from the insane to the care of those with tuberculosis. A commission was authorized to establish a State Sanatorium for Consumptives. A 700-acre site on the shore of Leech Lake near Walker was selected. The land was purchased in 1903, and the facility opened at the end of 1907.

By the summer, its full capacity of fifty-five patients had been reached. The cost per day per patient that first year was one dollar. Amenities included a piano and 250-volume library—largely stocked from donations by Twin Cities' women's clubs.[18]

Employee housing was inadequate and hiring domestic help was difficult, so some discharged patients were kept on as employees.

The superintendent said the sanatorium was set up to treat early cases of TB, often for six months to a year. It was not intended to be a custodial institution for far-advanced quiescent cases. The purpose of the institution was treatment and discharge back to society. Patients were admitted upon application by a physician and their home county commissioners had to guarantee payment of expenses. Discharge was voluntary and done without any formality.[19]

WILLMAR

CONCERN SHIFTED BACK TO CARE FOR INEBRIATES and a second state hospital for alcoholics was approved in 1907. A 500-acre farm was purchased in Willmar and the facility opened in 1912. Built to hold only fifty patients, the capacity was expanded two years later to house one hundred. Prohibition efforts decreased the need for an inebriate hospital, so services were expanded in 1917 to include custodial care for chronically insane patients from other hospitals. The name was changed in 1919 to Willmar State Asylum.

CAMBRIDGE

FARIBAULT WAS BECOMING OVERCROWDED with feeble-minded patients, so land was purchased on both banks of the Rum River at Cambridge. Functioning for the first two years as a subsidiary of Faribault, the first Cottage opened June 1, 1925. The main building opened in August of 1927, and it became a separate hospital—the Minnesota Colony for Epileptics. All epileptic patients of at least fair intelligence in the Faribault hospital were transferred to Cambridge, and other epileptic patients were admitted from throughout the state.[20]

The configuration of three receiving hospitals for the insane—St. Peter, Rochester and Fergus Falls—and three asylums—Anoka, Hastings and Willmar—continued for thirty years. In 1935, an additional facility in northern Minnesota was needed.

MOOSE LAKE

THE DECISION OF WHERE TO LOCATE a new state hospital in 1935 was convoluted and difficult. A commission was created and given the task of choosing a site in northern Minnesota near a population center with at least 640 acres of agricultural land. The legislature set the cost of the new hospital at 1.2 million dollars.

By September, the choice had been narrowed to the towns of Moose Lake or Virginia, both of whom offered inducements. Virginia supported its site by saying it could provide power and sewage services, saving over $200,000 in construction costs. The Commercial Club of Moose Lake countered by offering to pay costs in excess of what had been budgeted for land purchases—estimated to be about $12,000.[21]

September 7 was the application deadline for a potential Federal Works Progress Administration grant of $965,000.[22]

An application for the grant had been filed, but approval by Washington had been withheld pending approval of a site. A week after the due date, the commission announced that it had chosen Moose Lake. The state quickly went about acquiring the titles to twenty-seven pieces of land.[23]

The Virginia city attorney protested the decision, and two days later wired to Washington demanding an investigation.[24]

The WPA failed to grant the Moose Lake project, while approving $250,000 worth of projects in five other Minnesota institutions. Opposition by the town of Virginia precipitated the refusal. Construction plans went ahead, despite the lack of the federal grant, because the legislature had authorized full funding.[25]

Governor Olson paid a political price on the Iron Range for having approved the Moose Lake site. When he went to give a speech in Virginia in late October of that year, most aldermen refused to attend. The Virginia unit of the Farmer-Labor Party went on record against further assistance to the governor's campaign. Governor Olson made light of the situation, saying he believed that he might get shot if he came to Virginia, but had come because he decided that those who opposed him "couldn't shoot straight anyway."[26]

Acting on a request by the Virginia city attorney, the state attorney general ruled that the commission's records were open to public inspection. Virginia claimed that some landowners at Moose Lake were being pressured to sell, which the chair of the State Board of Control denied.[27]

A Virginia grocer filed a lawsuit seeking an injunction against buying land or beginning construction of the hospital. He claimed, in part, that the Moose Lake site was not located near a population center and raised several constitutional questions about how the bill came into law and how commission members had been appointed.[28] The Moose Lake Commercial Club called Virginia "poor sports,"[29] and a resident of Moose Lake filed a counter suit, claiming that the proposed Virginia site was unsuited to farming and was a wilderness.[30]

A state senator and representative from the Moose Lake area upped the ante by threatening a court action to test whether Virginia should be receiving tax monies from mines operating on land leased by the state. They claimed that state-owned land was exempt from taxes. Since mines were among the largest taxpayers in the state, this could have affected not only city revenues, but county and state tax collections as well. The Virginia attorney said the threats would have no effect on his client's effort to get a decision on the legality of the site selection.[31]

Moose Lake legislators bypassed the court maneuverings by introducing house and Senate bills confirming the site selection commission's decision.[32] The bill passed in the House just before the Christmas recess, with only two dissenting votes,[33] and it passed in the Senate on January 8.[34] Moose Lake opened in 1938 as the fourth hospital for the insane.

BRAINERD

To HOUSE A BURGEONING POPULATION of retarded children and adults, the Brainerd State School and Hospital was opened in 1958. At first it had only ninety patients, most of whom came from Cambridge State School and Hospital. Buildings were quickly added, and by 1965, with the addition of patients from Faribault, the population had grown to 1,330. Construction was said to have cost eighteen million dollars.

The Department of Public Welfare, which oversaw all state hospitals, directed in 1966 that residents be grouped by geographic area. This meant that during a two-week period, 1,250 residents had to be moved between buildings. There weren't enough staff to carry out all the tasks necessary, so volunteers assisted.[35]

ANCILLARY FACILITIES

A NUMBER OF OTHER STATE FACILITIES HOUSED feeble-minded, mentally ill, geriatric and TB patients. While not constructed as state hospitals, they served ancillary roles.

SANDSTONE

BEGINNING IN 1950, THE STATE LEASED the federal prison at Sandstone for nine years and used it to house ambulant male patients from other hospitals and patients admitted for alcoholism treatment from the eight northeastern Minnesota counties.[36]

The federal government reclaimed the facility about the time the final large state hospital opened in Brainerd in 1958.

Sauk Centre Home School for Girls

Beginning in 1911, delinquent girls committed by the court were sent to the Sauk Centre Home School for Girls. Children as young as eight years old were admitted.[37]

Commitments ended at age twenty-one. With the passage of the 1925 law authorizing sterilizations, inmates whose IQs placed them in the feeble-minded range were sent to Faribault after their twentieth birthday. They were sterilized and returned to Sauk Centre for convalescence.[38] Sterilization of these defective women was considered a necessary part of pre-discharge preparations.

Describing the population of the Faribault hospital in 1940, the super-intendent stated:

> The fifth group is made up of girls transferred to us from the State School for Delinquent Girls at Sauk Centre. This in-stitution is not one planned for the care of feeble-minded but some are found to be mentally defective after admission and these are committed to the custody of the State Board of Control. However, because of our lack of space, their training is completed at Sauk Centre and those considered suitable for placement are sent to us for sterilization.[39]

Overcrowding at Faribault led to using three cottages at the Sauk Cen-tre site in 1951 to care for severely retarded children.

Asylum for the Dangerously Insane

The Asylum for the Dangerously Insane opened in May 1911, on the grounds of St. Peter State Hospital. Two months later, it housed sixty-four patients in a building intended for fifty. It was built essentially as a jail, with barred cells. Over the years, both facilities at St. Peter shared administrators. Food raised on the grounds was consumed by both.

Inmates could be sent to the asylum by the court if found to be insane while under indictment or during a trial. When they recovered, they would be returned for trial. Anyone in a state prison alleged to be insane could be examined by the probate court and transferred to the asylum until his sanity was restored. If that occurred before his sentence was complete, he would be returned to prison. State hospital patients could be transferred to the asylum if found by the State Board of Control to have homicidal tendencies.[40]

The law left open the possibility of confinement for life. The decision of whether an inmate's sanity had been restored was left to the superintendent.

The asylum was criticized both for confining patients too much, and for not being secure enough. Several well-publicized escapes occurred in the 1920s and '30s. The second one included sixteen inmates and involved the St. Peter National Guard to aid in the search for them. By mid-century, pa-

Security hospital interior ca. 1950, courtesy of Nicollet County Historical Society. The Asylum for the Dangerously Insane was built and operated much like a prison for many years.

tients protested that the institution's name was demoralizing and bloodcurdling. The name was changed to the Minnesota Security Hospital in 1957.[41]

The security hospital had its own kitchen and served a diet heavy on vegetables. During World War II, sugar and coffee were non-existent. Only one slice of bread was provided for each meal, with one pat of butter at breakfast. Baked potatoes and prunes were staples for supper. Fruit and baked goods were unknown except for an occasional piece of cake, described as a leaden, doughy mess.

Recreation was limited to a few patients playing softball and getting exercise polishing the wooden floors by pulling blanketed sandbags, with ropes attached, up and down the halls. The need to keep patients locked in the building limited possible work tasks. Female patients embroidered, tatted, and knitted stockings. Males made rag carpets and laundry nets.[42]

Punishments were harsh in the 1940s and early '50s. Patients were put in straightjackets and stood against the barred windows, sometimes with the straps in back tied around the bars. For serious infractions, patients were given large doses of purgatives and tied down to a bed for a day or two. The harsh atmosphere led to frequent fights between patients and animosity between patients and staff.

Things improved during the late 1950s, including better diets, elimination of restraints, additional recreation and chaplain services.[43] The security hospital was the subject of the Governor's campaign in 1962, leading to additional improvements. Music therapy began, female nurses served the

Security hospital exterior ca. 1950, courtesy of Nicollet County Historical Society. Despite its forbidding appearance, several escapes took place.

wards, and patients' family members were allowed to visit. Curtains and pictures went up, the interior was painted and new lighting installed. Medical services greatly improved, and a patient self-governing program improved relationships between patients.[44]

Owatonna State School

The State Public School for Dependent and Neglected Children opened in Owatonna in 1885. It served as an orphanage until being phased out in 1945. For the next twenty-five years, the school provided academic and vocational programs for the educable mentally disabled.

The boys were quite active outdoors. The superintendent felt the need to contact the state health department about the safety of "... our state school boys capturing wild squirrels, gophers and rats and making pets of them."[45] Years later, when a newly caught pet squirrel died, it was sent to the state health department lab, who found no evidence of rabies.[46]

As local schools began to provide services for more children with disabilities, the Owatonna State School admitted more children with emotional and behavioral problems.[47] The range of medical and psychiatric needs are evidenced by the daily medications dispensed, including Thorazine, Equanil, Mebaral, Paradione, Phenobarbital and Dilantin.[48]

While it was housing the mentally disabled, the Owatonna School provided candidates for sterilization. In the 1950s, approval for sterilization of children at the Owatonna State School required psychological and medical approval. The request then was sent to the Public Welfare central office, who contacted the family to get consent. The central office ensured that the county welfare board made placement plans for the child. Before transfer to Faribault for the operation, staff at Owatonna discussed the question of sterilization with the "ward," in most cases showing them the consent papers their guardian had approved.[49]

Minnesota Children's Center

The Minnesota Children's Center was established in July 1945 to care for the children remaining in the Owatonna state school when it closed. Intended at first to be temporary, it became legally defined as a state institution for emotionally disturbed children in 1953. In 1958, it moved to North Hamline Avenue in St. Paul. By 1960, the former custodial approach was supplanted by treatment with an integration of psychiatry and social work.

During the 1960 biennium, it served children between the ages of nine and sixteen, for an average stay of eighteen months. Six patients were transferred to state hospitals, four to state correctional institutions, and eleven were discharged into the community.[50]

A fire in the center in February 1961 necessitated its closing. Half the children and staff went to Anoka, and the other half to Hastings.[51]

SHAKOPEE HOME FOR CHILDREN

THE SHAKOPEE HOME FOR CHILDREN was established in 1951, to provide additional capacity for mentally retarded girls. It evolved into a dual-purpose facility, providing penal rehabilitation and habilitation for severely retarded youngsters.[52]

Designed for up to thirty girls, it was staffed in part with inmates from the adjacent Women's Reformatory.[53]

LAKE OWASSO CHILDREN'S HOME

RAMSEY COUNTY CLOSED ITS PREVENTORIUM, which had been used to house children who had a parent with tuberculosis. The state took over the facility in 1955, operating it as a satellite facility of Faribault and later Cambridge State Hospital. During the 1961-1962 biennium, facilities were increased to 130 beds. Moderately retarded adult female patients were served until the facility closed in 1976.[54]

ANNEX FOR DEFECTIVE DELENQUENTS

RESPONDING TO DIFFICULTIES FARIBAULT was experiencing with the behavior of some of its male patients, the Annex For Defective Delinquents was opened in a wing of the St. Cloud Reformatory in 1956. It housed sixty-three higher-level mentally retarded boys and men. While in Faribault, the patients had been housed in a secure building with barred windows and given little access to hospital activities. They escaped, broke windows and injured aides. They left Faribault in chains and straightjackets.

At St. Cloud, they were housed in a dormitory and dayroom. An educational program stressed social living and vocational skills. They were taught to be truthful, dependable, responsible, and how to read and write. Lives of great men were presented and the chaplain talked of the virtues of religion and prayer.[55]

The Annex worked with County Welfare Boards to arrange for homes and jobs for patients who were discharged.[56] Seventy-five percent were discharged to the community, with very few requiring financial aid.

Objections were raised about incarcerating individuals in a state prison who had not been convicted of a crime. The Minnesota Bar Association adopted a resolution in 1962 urging repeal of the statute. A Governor's Advisory Committee on the Annex for Defective Delinquents issued a report that year recommending closing the facility. Declining numbers and the increased ability of other institutions for the mentally retarded would allow them to be supported in other settings.

OAK TERRACE NURSING HOME

HENNEPIN COUNTY OPENED the Glen Lake Sanatorium in 1914. By 1962, the facility had many empty beds, and the legislature authorized opening the facility as a state sanatorium and nursing home. The TB patients remaining at Ah-Gwan-Ching were transferred to Glen Lake. Geriatric patients were transferred from state hospitals to the section of the facility now called Oak Terrace Nursing Home. Three years later, part of the building was used as a training and rehabilitation center for retarded adolescents under the sponsorship of Twin Cities school districts. State services for TB patients ended in 1976, and the nursing home was closed in 1991. The building was demolished two years later and is now a golf course.[57]

LINO LAKES

THE MINNESOTA RESIDENTIAL TREATMENT CENTER at Lino Lakes opened in June 1963. Seventeen patients were transferred from the children's center at Glen Lake. Psychiatric services were provided for sixty children from throughout the state.[58]

Beginning in 1967, the center discontinued admitting adolescents, switching to children age five to twelve. From July 1966 to 1967, the center admitted ninety-seven children.[59]

In 1978, the institution was remodeled and converted to a level three, medium-security facility for adult males transferred from the state's higher-security prisons.[60]

CONTRUCTION SUMMARY

IF YOU HAD DRIVEN FROM FACILITY TO FACILITY and toured the grounds of each state hospital by car in the 1950s or 1960s, you would have seen the great efforts Minnesota was making to care for the mentally ill and retarded. Some buildings—like the facility in Fergus Falls—were huge, among the largest single public buildings in the state. Other grounds were so extensive and contained so many out buildings that they would have required a good part of a day to see.

New geriatric building Fergus Falls State Hospital ca. 1950, courtesy Minnesota Historical Society. This modern building plan was used at a number of other state hospitals to provide separate facilities to house the elderly. Formerly, they lived—and died—in the midst of the general population.

The idyllic lake side setting of Moose Lake and Willmar and the cozy river valley of Hastings were valuable properties. Architectural flourishes made gems of some buildings, and the placement of Anoka cottages around a central plaza was grand.

Behind those imposing façades, however, basic functions like water supplies, sewage, electric wiring and elevators deteriorated under the strain of overcrowding. Visitors didn't get beyond one or two rooms on the ground floors. Inadequate staffing created nightmare conditions behind the barred windows on the upper floors.

NOTES

1. Public Welfare Department. *A Review of the Laws of Minnesota Relating to the Feeble-minded.* Unpublished report, 1946 p. 1.
2. Erickson, William. "Establishing Minnesota's First Hospital for the Insane." *Minnesota History,* Summer 1992, p. 43.
3. Erickson, William. "Establishing Minnesota's First Hospital for the Insane." *Minnesota History,* Summer 1992, p. 45.
4. Seaquist, Elizabeth. "St. Peter State Hospital." *Minnesota Welfare,* Summer 1961, p. 6.
5. W. Erickson, MD. *The Great Charity: Minnesota's First Mental Hospital at St. Peter, St. Peter Regional Treatment Center.* 1991, p. 43.
6. Hahn, Ruth. *Oh, You Work at the Bughouse!* Taylor Publishing Co, Dallas. 1984, p. 97.
7. *Saint Peter Tribune,* November 24, 1880, p. 2.
8. *The Evolution of State Operated Services,* Minnesota Department of Human Services, ca. 2005.
9. Wells, Lloyd. "Rural Psychiatry on the Nineteenth-Century Frontier: the Career of Jacob Bowers." *Perspectives in Biology and Medicine* 24:2, 270-283.
10. *Quarry Hill Park, In Years Gone By.* Quarry Hill Nature Center Library.
11. Knight G. *First Biennial Report School for Imbeciles.* 1882, pp. 11-14.
12. *Minnesota School for Feeble-Minded and Colony for Epileptics Farbault and Colony for Epileptics Cambridge,* June 30, 1932, p. 2.
13. *Fergus Falls Daily Journal,* July 25, 1890, p. 3.
14. *Fergus Falls Daily Journal,* July 30, 1890, p. 3.
15. *First Annual Report of State Hospital for Crippled and Deformed Children.* 1898, Gillette Biennial Reports.
16. Stanchfield, Margaret. *History of Anoka State Hospital.* Thesis, 1948 Faribault Published Reports.
17. *Second Biennial Report of the Minnesota State Board of Visitors for Public Institutions.* 1910, p. 12.
18. Oliver, Skip. *A Brief History of the Minnesota State Sanatorium.* June 1982, p. 5.

19. *Quarterly Conference of Executive Officers of the State Institutions.* 192,9 p. 25.
20. *Minnesota School for Feeble-Minded and Colony for Epileptics Farbault and Colony for Epileptics Cambridge,* June 30, 1928, p. 9.
21. *Virginia Daily Enterprise,* September 17, 1935 p. 1.
22. *Virginia Daily Enterprise,* September 7, 1935 p. 1.
23. *Virginia Daily Enterprise,* September 17, 1935 p. 1.
24. *Virginia Daily Enterprise,* September 26, 1935 p. 1.
25. *Virginia Daily Enterprise,* October 1, 1935 p. 1; October 3 p. 1.
26. *Virginia Daily Enterprise,* October 22, 1935 pp. 1, 4.
27. *Virginia Daily Enterprise,* October 29, 1935 p. 1.
28. *Virginia Daily Enterprise,* November 2, 1935 p. 1, 4.
29. *Virginia Daily Enterprise,* November 5, 1935 p. 1.
30. *Virginia Daily Enterprise,* November 14, 1935 pp. 1, 4.
31. *Virginia Daily Enterprise,* December 3, 1935 pp. 1, 3.
32. *Virginia Daily Enterprise,* December 11, 1935 p. 1.
33. *Virginia Daily Enterprise,* December 20, 1935 p. 1.
34. *Virginia Daily Enterprise,* January 8, 1936 p. 1.
35. *Centennial Edition Brainerd Daily Dispatch* ,1971, brainderdhistory.com.
36. "Welfare Report Fall-Winter, 1958" p. 52.
37. Control Board, Published Records. "History of the State Board of Control 1902-1922."
38. "Faribault Record of Sterilizations."
39. Engberg, E. "The Treatment of Mental Defectives in Minnesota." *Minnesota Medicine* vol. 23, pp. 335- 338, May 1940. Public Welfare Feeble-Minded Miscellaneous, MHS.
40. MN Statute 1907, Chapter 338.
41. Seaquist, Elizabeth. "St. Peter State Hospital." *Minnesota Welfare,* Summer 1961, p. 39.
42. "Monthly Report, St. Peter January 1923," St. Peter SH Collection, Archives MN State University, Mankato.
43. Hopkins, Harlan. "Seventeen Years in Retrospect," *MSH Eagle,* November 1955, Security Hospital scrapbooks.
44. Morse, Ken. "MSH Through the Changing '60s." *MSH Eagle,* November 1970, Security Hospital scrapbooks.
45. Letter, June 29, 1959, Owatonna State School Administrative Records.
46. Owatonna State School Administrative Records, July 20, 1965.
47. Owatonna State School Administrative Records, July 20, 1965.
48. Owatonna State School Administrative Records, November 1956.
49. Owatonna State School, Sterilization letters, 1954-1958.
50. "Welfare Report Fall-Winter, 1960," pp. 50, 51.
51. "MN Welfare report, 1962," p. 54.
52. "MN Welfare Report Winter, 1968," p. 54.
53. "MN Welfare Report Fall-Winter, 1958," p. 58.
54. "MN Welfare Report, 1962," p. 54.
55. Dr. Harlan Paine. November 7, 1954, Faribault Superintendent's Correspondence.

56. "MN Welfare Report Fall-Winter, 1958," p. 58.
57. www.placeography.org.
58. "MN Welfare Report Winter, 1964," p. 51.
59. "MN Welfare Report Winter, 1968," p. 48.
60. www.doc.state.mn.us/facilities/linolakes.

CHAPTER TWO

ASYLUMS

As MINNESOTA WAS BEING SETTLED, there were no facilities to care for disturbed people. An affluent family might send a family member to a private asylum in the East, but most stayed with their families. If community members became frightened by an individual's behavior, that person was sent to jail. Another place many differently acting people ended up in was poor houses. The state Board of Corrections and Charities surveyed county poor houses in 1883. Of 624 inmates found throughout the state, sixty were found to be "idiots, imbeciles and epileptic."[1]

Mentally ill individuals often needed an asylum—a place of safety. Patients coming into the state hospitals during the early years demonstrated the lack of care they'd received in their home communities. An 1896 report stated that all the women patients admitted to state hospitals showed signs of disease. A number were emaciated and the majority poorly nourished.[2]

Hallway St. Peter State Hospital ca. 1910, courtesy Minnesota Historical Society.

Lower flat south sickroom, St. Peter ca. 1895, courtesy of Nicollet County Historical Society. In the earliest days, patients who could control their behavior lived in
surroundings better than the homes many of them came from.

Photographs from the early 1900s at St. Peter State Hospital show hallways and day rooms that were very appealing. Rocking chairs are nestled
between end tables holding plants. Graceful curtains adorn the windows
and pictures are on the walls. The atmosphere appears genteel and welcom-
ing. Rochester State Hospital grounds included a beautiful formal garden.

State hospital patients who could control themselves lived in an environment that may have been more refined than the simple rural homes they'd lived
in. The upper floors of hospitals were utilized for disturbed and violent patients,
with barred windows and little on the wards that could be thrown or broken.

Hospital superintendents complained in 1896:

> A great deal has been said and written about the improve-
> ment in the care of the insane during the last twenty years,
> and the name "Asylum" is gradually giving place everywhere

to that of "Hospital," and continuous and earnest effort is being made to make them really hospitals; but we cannot shut our eyes to the fact that at least sixty percent of the population of the state institutions are chronic cases, of fair physical health, so that they require very little nursing, the majority of them harmless, but demented and often filthy in habits. Consequently our institutions, in spite of the name we may apply to them, are to a great extent still asylums for a class of people that is simply kept there because there is no suitable place to care for it elsewhere.[3]

From the beginning, state hospitals served senile elderly patients who now go to nursing homes. Because there was no effective medical treatment,

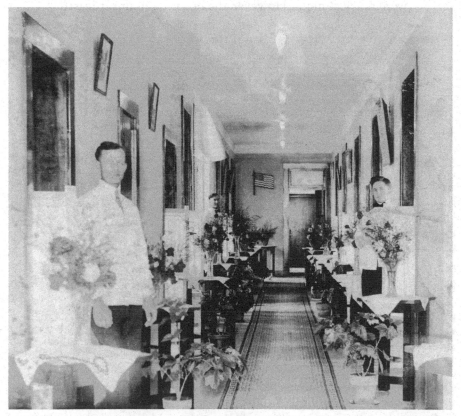

Lower flat south hallway, St. Peter State Hospital ca. 1895, courtesy of Nicollet County Historical Society.

people with epilepsy and the end stages of syphilis were also sent to be cared for until they died.

Stating that the majority of patients being admitted were over fifty years old, staff at St. Peter complained in 1900 that:

> These figures show that progressive tendency (most marked during the past five years) to make our state hospitals asylums for feeble-minded old people, whose personal habits make their care irksome upon their relatives; and the degree of mental disturbance necessary to bring about this transfer from the home to the hospital is growing less every year. We have had men and women committed who were paralyzed and helpless, and who were said to be insane because they were noisy at night. However, the real though unexpressed

Front lawn, Rochester State Hospital ca. 1900, courtesy Minnesota Historical Society This was part of the hospital's biennial report. In addition to a large, imposing building, these extensive grounds would have conveyed to visitors the state's support for the insane.

reason for the commitment of this class of cases is that they
require care because they are filthy . . . the present disposition
in this state to gradually remove from the hospitals all the
quiet, well-behaved chronic patients who do the domestic
work of the institution is going to add to our difficulties . . ."[4]

A considerable effort was made by the early state hospitals to understand mental illnesses. The staff at St. Peter carefully compiled a running
record of the "Alleged Causes of Insanity" occasioned by their patients. By
1888, they had admitted 4,820 patients during their first twenty-two years
of operation. No history of causation was known in 1,799 of the cases. In-
temperance was the most frequent cause with 242 cases, followed closely
by epilepsy with 234. Injury to the head trailed with ninety-three. Syphilis
was noted in five cases.

These causes of mental dysfunction are recognizable today. Others vary
in modern eyes from questionable causes, such as general ill health in 216
cases, to the laughable—masturbation for 185 patients. Other examples appear bizarre to us, including indigestion for five people, and single cases of
avarice, consulting a fortuneteller, excommunication and political excitement.[5] (Although some people might wish to be able to commit others today
for that last condition.)

It didn't take long for state hospitals to realize they could do little to
improve the functioning of many patients. As patient populations continued
to grow, the term "asylum" took on a new meaning, distinguishing facilities
providing only custodial care, not treatment. The State Board of Visitors for
Public Institutions found, in 1910, that the state hospital system was 600
patients over capacity. Concerned about overcrowding that resulted in diminished care, they stated: "But the outstanding fact is that for many years
the state of Minnesota, while claiming to make provision for its insane, has
really never done so."

They divided the insane into the categories of acute—an illness of less
than two years in duration—and chronic. They advocated that every means
known to science should be used to treat acute patients, while chronic patients needed only custodial care. Anoka and Hastings were intended for

these purposes and opened in 1900, with Willmar added seventeen years later.[6]

Perhaps the biggest difference between the receiving hospitals and asylums was the movement of some patients in and out of the former, with little expectation of patients being discharged from the latter. Neither type of facility utilized individual treatment plans or provided annual physicals. Both involved as many patients as possible in the work needed to run the hospital, which they considered to be beneficial. Keeping patient behavior under control was a concern in all the institutions and the limited techniques available were used to calm patients and prevent them from injuring themselves or others.

NOTES

1. McClure, Ethel. "An Unlamented Era: County Poor Farms in Minnesota." *Minnesota History* 38, pp. 369 -70, December 1963.
2. *Ninth Biennial Report of the Board of Trustees and Officers of the Minnesota Hospitals for Insane.* July 31, 1896, p. 20.
3. *Tenth Biennial Report of the Board of Trustees and Officers of the Minnesota Hospitals for Insane.* July 31, 1898, p. 157.
4. *Eleventh Biennial Report of the Board of Trustees and Officers of the Minnesota Hospitals for Insane.* July 31, 1900, p. 18.
5. *Fifth Biennial Report of the Board of Trustees and Officers of the Minnesota Hospital for Insane.* July 31, 1888, pp. 56-58.
6. *Second Biennial Report of the Minnesota State Board of Visitors for Public Institutions.* 1910, pp. 8-10.

Chapter Three

Treatment Centers

A Promising Beginning

In their 1900 report, the trustees of the state hospital system stated that:

> The theory of our state hospitals is the treatment and cure of the insane. That is the purpose for which they were established, and is that for which the people pay. This state may feel justly proud of its liberality and the work that is being done at its expense in our charitable institutions for the care and treatment of the insane, and it is probably true that not one in ten of the inmates our insane hospitals have received so careful treatment in their own homes, or ever enjoyed there the accommodation and comforts that the state affords them in such hospitals.[1]

From the time they opened, all the state hospitals did what they could to improve the patients' functioning. Prior to the advent of psychotrophic drugs in the 1950s, there were no medical interventions available that enabled patients who were out of control or out of touch with reality to consistently function. State hospitals were faced with large numbers of patients who often got worse. There was little they could do.

The advantages of a caring environment and activity were demonstrated as early as 1822. The McLean Asylum in Boston utilized a system of moral management, including chess, nine-pins, sawing wood and gardening. Restraints and physical punishment were not allowed.[2]

These humane efforts were later swamped by the ever increasing numbers of patients.

When it had been open for ten years, the Rochester State Hospital adopted a philosophy of not restraining patients. The superintendent proudly reported that there were some months when none of the male patients had been restrained. He also began an open door policy for one ward and several day rooms. [3]

When Fergus Falls opened in 1890, the superintendent declared that, "... treatment will be directed not to restraint and punishment, but to cure. Thus games and recreation of all kinds—especially that kind which requires vigorous exercise—will form an important part of the treatment. Good food, exercise, regular house and habits—all these play as important a part in the care of lunacy as they do in the cure of other diseases."[4]

When requesting additional funds, Fergus Falls, in 1894, pointed out that northern Minnesota winters caused farm families to be socially isolated. This was said to be an important cause of insanity because the brain was starved and the normal mental condition became unbalanced from a continual

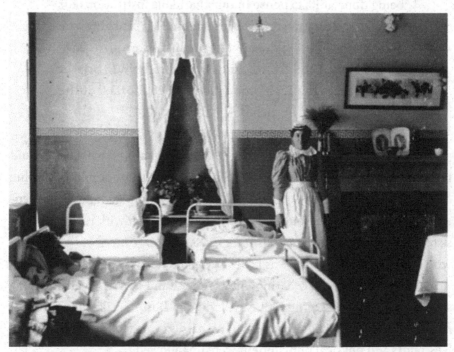

Nurse with patient at Fergus Falls State Hospital ca. 1910, courtesy Minnesota Historical Society. With curtains, pictures on the walls and a fireplace, this was a pleasant room.

monotony of existence. Such patients were said to recover quickly where pleasure and amusement formed a share of their daily existence.[5]

Fergus Falls reported on how well its early treatment regimen was working. They found that most of the patients who were discharged as recovered had gained weight while in the hospital. They thus concluded:

> This goes to show that diet is an important portion of the treatment of insanity and that insanity is a disease of debility. There is no question connected with the care and treatment of the insane that is more worthy of attentive study than diet. Milk is the main special diet in the hospital and we prefer to give it hot, but great care is taken to prevent it from being scalded. It should always be imbibed slowly. Through the complementary forces of rest and milk we have been able to largely dispense with every kind of physical restraint whatever.[6]

Ward at Christmas St. Peter State Hospital ca. 1900, courtesy of Nicollet County Historical Society. Perhaps the room was staged for the photo, nonetheless, the bedding appears adequate and a cloth is on the table.

The rest they referred to consisted of "protective sheets" that kept patients in bed. This enabled them to provide patients with the "bed treatment," which they said was the foundation of the modern method of caring for the insane. They claimed a recovery rate of over seventy percent and death rate of only two to five percent.[7]

Six years later, Fergus Falls had added homeopathic treatments, cited as the cause for very satisfactory results in treating acute insanity. During the first eight years the hospital was open, over 400 patients were sent out recovered.[8]

The virtues of outdoor labor were extolled in the 1892 Biennial Report of the Minnesota Hospitals for the Insane, which stated that patients ". . . gain rest and quiet by healthful occupation in the open air. They become interested in this work, and are thereby diverted for a time from their melancholy vagaries. The get sufficiently wearied for recuperative sleep, nature's best curative agent."[9]

Work would continue to be considered therapeutic. This provided a rationale for not paying patients. In the 1920s, it was termed "occupational work." An improvement at St. Peter involved having teachers or helpers bring handwork tasks onto the wards for patients who couldn't be allowed to go to the "occupational rooms." By 1932, St. Peter used the term "occupational therapy" to report that 250 patients were making shirts, overalls, toweling, rugs, toys and knick-knacks.[10]

Adequate nutrition helped many new Rochester patients improve. The majority of women patients admitted to Rochester during the biennium ending July 1896 were malnourished. Thirty-two were emaciated and exhausted from delirium. Patients who refused to eat were force-fed, producing better results than the former policy of waiting until the patient was ready to eat, which had resulted in most of them dying. Nearly all patients had to be urged to eat. Rochester utilized a separate kitchen in the receiving building that could cater to special diets and the individual tastes of patients. This was said to be a great help.[11]

Twenty percent of the first forty patients admitted to Rochester were discharged in less than a year, and fifty percent in less than five years. Only five percent stayed until they died.[12]

NOTES

1. *Eleventh Biennial Report of the Board of Trustees and Officers of the Minnesota Hospitals for Insane.* July 31, 1900, p. 6.

2. Edward Shorter. *A History of Psychiatry*, John Wiley & sons, New York, 1997. p. 45.

3. *Fifth Biennial Report of the Board of Trustees and Officers of the Minnesota Hospital for Insane.* p. 106, 107.

4. *Fergus Falls Daily Journal*, July 25, 1890, p. 3.

5. *Eighth Biennial Report of the Board of Trustees and Officers of the Minnesota Hospitals for Insane.* July 31, 1894, pp. 166, 167.

6. *Seventh Biennial Report of the Board of Trustees and Officers of the Minnesota Hospitals for Insane.* July 31, 1892, p. 160.

7. *Seventh Biennial Report of the Board of Trustees and Officers of the Minnesota Hospital for Insane*, p. 161.

8. *Tenth Biennial Report of the Board of Trustees and Officers of the Minnesota Hospitals for Insane.* July 31, 1898, p. 154.

9. *Seventh Biennial Report, Minnesota Hospitals for the Insane.* July 1892.

10. "Monthly Reports," St. Peter SH, January 1923, April 1932, St. Peter SH Collection, Archives MN State University, Mankato.

11. *Ninth Biennial Report, Minnesota Hospitals for Insane.* July 31, 1896.

12. Wells, Lloyd. "Rural Psychiatry on the Nineteenth-Century Frontier: the Career of Jacob Bowers." *Perspectives in Biology and Medicine*, 1981, vo.l 24, pp. 270-83.

CHAPTER FOUR
OVERCROWDING

THE EXAMPLES GIVEN ABOVE OF THE BENEFITS of exercise, diet and a safe environment occurred in the nineteenth century. As more and more patients were admitted after 1900, the staff and facilities became overwhelmed. A calm, low-key environment could no longer be provided. One influx of patients occurred shortly after the end of World War I, when one-hundred-and-seventy-six former servicemen were confined in the Rochester State Hospital. The federal government sent thirty-five dollars a month for their care once their service status was determined.[1]

Over the next fifty years, wards became progressively crowded. Funding and staffing were difficult during both world wars and the intervening

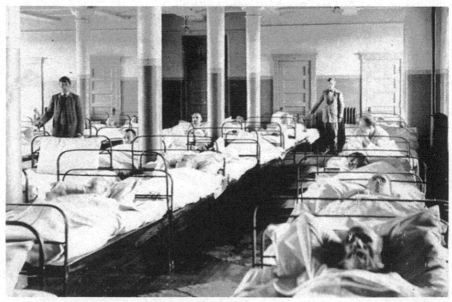

Fergus Falls State Hospital ca. 1900, courtesy Minnesota Historical Society. In later years, conditions got worse than this, with patients having to make due without sheets or pillows, and with torn blankets. Mattresses were rarely changed, and some patients on these wards were bedridden and incontinent.

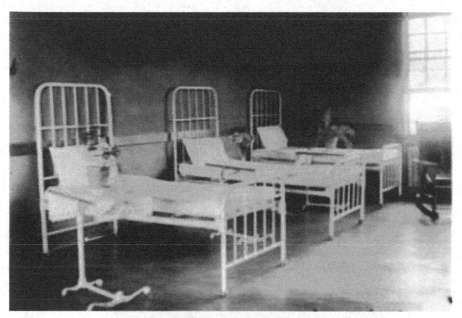

Beds in lower flat south, St. Peter State Hospital ca. 1920, courtesy of Nicollet County Historical Society. The room isn't jammed with beds, but is certainly bare.

depression. It was noted, in 1930, that an increasing number of families were unable to care for senile or infirm relatives. This placed an additional burden on the hospital.[2]

By 1938, the percentage of patients admitted who were over sixty years old grew to thirty percent at St. Peter.[3]

Photographs from the 1940s show wards with no curtains or pictures. Benches or chairs line the walls. There was barely room to walk between beds, and some patients slept in hallways or unheated porches.

Rochester responded to the overcrowding by setting up 142 cots each night, putting them in hallways and any other available space.[4] Dayrooms were also converted to dormitory space.[5] A 1947 report on construction needs acknowledged that Rochester State Hospital was so overcrowded that patients had to sleep in hallways. 250 men were living in a building unfit for human habitation.[6]

St. Peter utilized folding cots that could be stored under beds during the day. This was more convenient that piling cots in one corner of the room, and mattresses in another corner.[7]

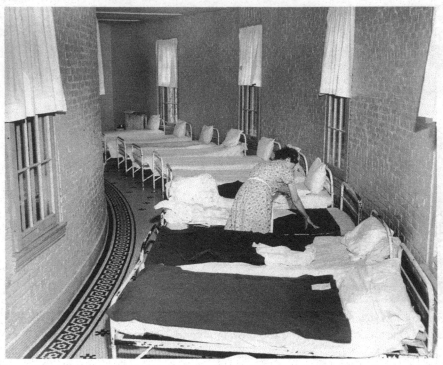

Overcrowded sleeping areas, Fergus Falls State Hospital ca. 1948, courtesy Minnesota Historical Society. Several state hospitals used dayrooms, setting up beds each night.

What the hospitals could and had to do to survive was control behavior. For the first half of the twentieth century, there were no interventions that would produce permanent improvement and allow patients to be discharged. Instead, treatment decisions focused on diminishing the most severe symptoms—aggression to self or others, agitation and deep depression. With permanent options not available, short term improvement was considered a success.

The need for methods of sedating patients is documented in patient death records. Exhaustion due to mania caused deaths from the earliest records until as late as 1948, when it led to the death of two younger patients at Moose Lake.[8]

Early sedatives used included laudanum and sodium barbital. It was noted that these contributed to deterioration and, if heavily sedated, patients could develop pneumonia.

Mechanical restraints were the most common method of controlling unruly patients. The use of restraints became so ubiquitous at Anoka that patients were brought to visit relatives while in restraints.[9]

NOTES

1. *Biennial Report, Hospitals and Asylums for the Insane of Minnesota.* June 30, 1922, p. 1.

2. *Biennial Report, Hospitals and Asylums for the Insane of Minnesota.* June 30, 1922, p. 17.

3. *Biennial Report Of the Hospitals for the Insane of Minnesota.* June 30, 1938, p. 40.

4. "Visitation Record," Rochester State Hospital. May 10, 1946, Social Security Department.

5. "Visitation Record," Rochester State Hospital. August 14, 1946, Social Security Department.

6. *Report of the Interim Committee on State Institution Buildings*, Legislative Reference Library.

7. "Monthly report," St. Peter SH, June 1935, St. Peter SH Collection, Archives Minnesota State University, Mankato.

8. "Moose Lake Admission record."

9. "Anoka staff conference minutes, 1948."

CHAPTER FIVE

GENETIC JAILS

THE TURN OF THE TWENTIETH CENTURY was a period of great change in the United States. Immigration swelled, with the majority of new arrivals coming from southern, rather than northern, Europe. The First World War hurled humanity into a previously unimaginable cataclysm of conflict. Science and technology produced incredible new inventions—the automobile, telephone, radio, and airplane.

These two elements—the uncertainty produced by change and the reverence for science—combined to produce a fertile environment for notions of human genetics. Modern science, endorsed by leaders in religion, business and politics, proclaimed not only that the human race could be improved, but that it must be protected from the insidious effects of the newly discovered defective "germ plasm."

Americans had long been willing to stomp on the lives of a minority population to protect the interests of the majority. Examples during this time period were the local committees that sprang up during the First World War to enforce community standards of patriotism.

Modern genetics provided a seemingly irrefutable argument—defective people should not be allowed to reproduce. Early proponents suggested three solutions: segregation, sterilization and euthanasia. The last was applied only in Nazi Germany, the second was controversial and only partly put in place, but the first—segregation—became embedded in the public conscience.

State hospitals in Minnesota and across the country took on the role of housing the insane and feeble-minded. Commitment laws sent people into institutions for life. No longer was it the hospital's primary task to treat and discharge patients. Once committed, even if for a temporary condition such as post-partum depression, patients were in forever.

These policies resulted in steady increases in hospital populations. Habitual underfunding coupled with few treatment options led to horrific conditions.

Responding to attempts to pass legislation creating industries within state institutions in 1923 and 1926, the Minnesota State Federation of Labor decided to conduct some research. Permission was obtained from the State Board of Control to conduct inspection tours. All state penal and hospital facilities except Cambridge, Gillette, Ah-Gwah-Ching, and Owatonna were visited with no advance warning during the winter of 1926-1927.

The purpose of the visits was to determine whether—as had been charged in the legislature—a large number of inmates were idle and lacked opportunities to engage in tasks that would assist in their rehabilitation. These labor leaders made it clear that they opposed the use of inmate labor to produce articles to be sold on the open market in competition with free labor.

Once their inspections began, their concerns quickly broadened from the question of competitive labor to comments on overcrowding, rehabilitation and prevention. They found that Faribault was "horribly overcrowded." They criticized the lack of segregation of patients in receiving mental hospitals, reporting,

> Facilities at present are such that the superintendents of these institutions are not able to grade the patients so as to separate them in accordance with their mental condition. It is apparent to anyone who investigates these institutions that the mingling of those not totally mental defective with those that are in a very low grade of mentality is not conducive to the rehabilitation and cure of the former.[1]

The Minnesota State Federation of Labor recommended construction of another hospital to house chronic patients and concluded that with the exception of the St. Cloud reformatory, those inmates who were capable of working had been assigned tasks. There was no need for the state to authorize setting up additional factories within state institutions.

Voicing concern about the growing numbers in all institutions, they spoke strongly in support of research to prevent mental deficiency:

> No means, in the opinion of your committee, are too drastic
> to prevent the propagation of the feeble-minded, the imbe-
> cile, and the idiotic . . . we desire to suggest that the causes
> for the ever increasing number of misfits of society should
> receive more attention than the question of what to do with
> them after they become misfits. . . . Locking up the morally
> and mentally defective is very simple, but the rapid increase
> of this class should be a challenge to our claim of being a
> Christian, as well as a civilized community.[2]

They had high praise for the leaders of the institutions, saying, "Every man and woman heading one of these institutions is doing everything possible in the interest of those committed to their charge as far as the facilities furnished them will permit."[3]

Thus, to some inside and outside the institutional system, the response to overcrowded state hospitals was not to treat and release people, but to prevent their birth. Moral and Christian concerns were not focused on those already in the hospitals, who had lost their rights and freedom.

The pernicious effects of genetic teachings were felt outside the institutions as well. Poorly conducted surveys demonstrated that alarming numbers of defectives in the general population were breeding. Recessive bad genes could be hidden in seemingly normal people, and individuals were encouraged to comb through family histories to demonstrate their genetic fitness.

The leading eugenicist in Minnesota wrote that, "The first law of heredity of mentality is that 'Two mentally defective parents will produce only mentally defective offspring.' The second law is that 'No imbecile is born except of parents, who if not mentally defective themselves, both carry mental defect in their germ-plasm.'"[4]

Eugenicists made it clear that this was a widespread problem that all members of the public should be aware of. Charles F. Dight wrote, in 1922:

But the breeding of defectives and the vicious is not confined to notorious cases. The fact is that just as we have people among us who are carriers of disease germs such as that
of typhoid fever, though in good health, so we have persons
by the millions who though normal in their mentalities
carry in the blood—their germ-plasm—the hereditary de-
terminers of bad physical and mental qualities or traits
which may by bad marriage matings come out by heredity
in a certain per cent of their descendants as insanity, mental
incompetency, avarice and inclination to criminality.[5]

The flip side of genealogical studies was the stigma assigned to any relative of a defective person. The only proof of the presence of defective germ
plasm was an insane or feeble-minded person, who tainted all family members. Not only was there a social stigma, but the rest of the family members'
worthiness to marry was impaired. Eugenics trumpeted that, "Human society consists of a great mingling of people of different strains, some good,
some bad, and of all intermediate grades. This requires that great care be
taken in selecting a marriage mate if those are to be avoided who are themselves defective or who carry defective germ-plasm, and may, therefore, pass
defects on to their offspring. Such people exist by the millions."[6]

Family members' attitudes about committed insane patients were cru-
cial. A feeble-minded person could get out and have their rights restored if
they could prove they were now functional. A committed insane person
didn't have to prove they had recovered, but they needed someone to agree
to be responsible for them before they could be discharged.

Given the common belief that family members were genetically
tainted, who would want an insane person in their home? It was bad enough
when an odd family member was whisked off and disappeared. Perhaps people would forget after a while. To bring them back home was like raising a
banner in the front yard that said, "Our family is defective."

The result was that many people committed as insane, for whatever
reason, had no hope of ever leaving. Perhaps a doctor at the state hospital
would go to bat for a new patient, demanding that their commitment be

Shack, St. Peter State Hospital ca. 1950s, courtesy of Nicollet County Historical Society. A liberty system at St. Peter allowed patients freedom during the day. A number of them built small shacks on the hospital grounds.

revisited by the court. That happened in a few cases when people came into the hospital and showed no symptoms of mental illness. How they managed to keep their composure when immersed in such a horrific process is a mystery. For the rest of those committed, becoming independent and fully capable resulted in hospital privileges, but no discharge.

I remember seeing a rack of band uniforms in the basement of a state hospital building. It was explained to me that there had been a patient marching band that would participate in local communities' parades. Despite being capable of independently running complex farm operations or performing in a marching band, patients were not released.

Another example occured between 1920 and the hospital's close, when high functioning patients at St. Peter built 100 "shacks." Using lumber scrounged from the hospital dump and tin cans cut up and flattened for shingles and siding, patients with liberty privileges created homes for themselves and lived in them during the day. Some operated small business from their shack, selling eggs or minnows to people from town.[7]

The demonstrated ability to build one's own home, live alone and operate a small business didn't lead to being discharged until the 1950s.

I was told by old-time staff members that local papers sometimes ran obituaries for patients at the time they were committed. The sense of shame was so strong that an obituary explained the family member's absence. They were never coming back, and were in effect dead to the outside world.

NOTES

1. Lawson, Starkey, Fullerton, Munkeby. "Minnesota's State Institutions, 1927." www.mnddc.org/past/pdf/20s/27/27-mn-fed-labor-mn-state-inst.pdf.
2. *ibid.*
3. *ibid.*
4. Dight, Charles F. *Human Thoroughbreds: Why Not?*, 1922.
5. *ibid.*
6. *ibid.*
7. *The Old Times*, Dec 1994, p. 1B, St. Peter Regional Treatment Center Archives.

CHAPTER SIX
THE EUGENICS MOVEMENT

Beginning in the late 1800s, newly discovered principles of genetics were adapted by those with a social agenda. What would come to be called "eugenics" called for maintaining the purity of America's Nordic people. It was both a racial ideology and an effort to prevent the birth of the unfit, wrapped in a patina of pseudo-science.

Northern Europeans, who dominated American economics and politics at the end of the nineteenth century, saw themselves as superior. Eugenics held great appeal because it confirmed their superiority and provided a means for maintaining it.

Early on, eugenics spoke of two main efforts—encouraging suitable marriages and child bearing by those deemed worthy (positive eugenics) and preventing defectives from procreating (negative eugenics). Alexander Graham Bell quickly became uncomfortable with negative eugenics, and urged a more positive approach. Among the upper class, the notion of being told whom to marry and the encouragement to have lots of children never caught on. Eugenics came to be associated with preventing unwanted progeny.

Liberal Protestants helped lay the groundwork for eugenics. The Reverend Oscar McCulloch, who served the Plymouth Congregational Church in Indianapolis beginning in 1877, preached the Social Gospel and through his own and his church's efforts founded many local philanthropic institutions. He studied a client's extended family members and found hundreds with hereditary degeneracy. Presenting his findings about the Ishamael family, he came to decry indiscriminate benevolence. He proposed ending public relief, limiting private relief, and getting hold of the children.

Indiana passed a law in 1889 that established county boards empowered to gather family histories and take charge of the children of incompetent parents. Scientific philanthropy would then ignore the parent's predicament. Rev. McCulloch's efforts were so well thought of that he was named president of the National Conference of Charities and Correction in 1891.[1]

Support for eugenics was not limited to liberal Protestants. In a 1915 paper entitled "Jewish Eugenics," Rabbi Max Reichler argued that eugenic rules were part of Biblical and Rabbinical laws. The main object of marriage was reproduction of the human race and augmentation of the favored stock. Thus, marriage by defectives such as epileptics, the deaf and dumb, and the lame and blind was prohibited.[2]

The American Eugenics Society published a catechism in 1927, formed in a question and answer format. Included were the following:

> **Does eugenics mean less sympathy for the unfortunate?**
> Eugenics does not mean less sympathy for the unfortunate; it does mean fewer unavoidable unfortunates with which to divide a sympathy which should be more fully and effectively expended on the inevitable unfortunates. This is a true kindness, both to the victims and to society.
>
> **In what way is crime a concern of eugenics?** The elements of personality—e.g. lack of strong social instincts or lack of self-control—which lie at the bottom of many crimes have a hereditary element. To understand the recidivist it is important to know his constitution as it may be inferred from a study of his family as a whole.
>
> **What is meant by negative eugenics?** To rid the race of those likely to transmit the dysgenic tendencies to which they are subject. To decrease the need for charity of a certain form. To reduce taxes. To help alleviate misery and suffering. To do what Nature would do under natural conditions, but more humanely. Sterilization is not a punitive measure. It is strictly protective.

Who should be sterilized? Such criminals, paupers, insane, feeble-minded, epileptics, rapists and other defectives who can be proved to have inherited such defects as make them incapable of leading ordinarily normal lives, and who, unless sterilized, are likely to transmit their defects to their children.

What are segregation farms good for? These farms have been recommended instead of jails for persons actively or potentially a menace to society and not requiring unusual restraint. Many of these people need custodial care for their own benefit as well as for that of the state by preventing their reproduction and other damage to society.

What is meant by positive eugenics? This deals with the forces which tend upward, or with the furtherance of human evolution. Encouraging the best endowed to produce four or more children per family, encouraging the study of eugenics by all, etc., are positive eugenics.[3]

Eugenics developed two major efforts. On the national level this played out along racial lines, culminating in limiting immigration by non-Nordic people. On the state level, concern was focused on improving society by limiting the birth of the unfit. This is not to say that there wasn't racial bias within the state level eugenic movement. In some states, African Americans and Native Americans were more likely to score poorly on IQ tests, both because of the cultural bias of the tests and their having had less access to education. As a result, they were disproportionately sterilized.[4]

Individuals supported the eugenics movement for a variety of reasons. There were a few Catholic priests and Jewish rabbis who were members of the American Eugenics Society as late as 1930. Looking back, we can see the panoply spawned by eugenics. At the time, it was possible to focus on one aspect of the movement and ignore others.

Eugenics was supported by some of the nation's most respected and educated figures. Financial backing for eugenic research came from the

Carneige Institution and John D. Rockefeller.[5] Early efforts were associated with the secretary of the U.S. Department of Agriculture, while Harvard University taught eugenics and the American Medical Association published its findings. Former president Theodore Roosevelt wrote in 1913, "I agree with you . . . that society has no business to permit degenerates to reproduce their kind . . ."[6] Vice President Charles Curtis's picture appeared on eugenic publications.[7]

This might have stayed the ranting of a few racists, were it not for eugenics' seeming validity. Voluminous "research" was carried out, and the results were widely trumpeted. Valid genetic research was combined with flawed research designs and vague definitions to reach pre-determined conclusions. For example, prison inmate records were examined. When it was found that a disproportionate percentage were African American, it was concluded that African Americans were a criminal race.

During World War I, heavily cultrally biased intelligence tests were given. It was discovered that fewer than one percent of Northern Europeans failed the test, while forty-seven percent of other whites and eighty-nine percent of African Americans were shown to have a mental capacity less than that of a thirteen-year-old.[8] These findings provided "proof" of Nordic superiority and were widely disseminated to state legislatures and Congress.

Eugenic research also included studying family histories. In 1904, the Carnegie Institution's Station for Experimental Evolution at Cold Spring Harbor opened. In addition to studying animals and plants, it set up the Eugenics Record Office (ERO) to register the genetic backgrounds of all Americans. The information would be collected from charitable institutions, insurance companies and colleges. The ERO would also promote legislation for the forced prevention of unwanted progeny.[9]

Some of this research was conducted in state hospitals and prisons, but field workers gathered ancestry statistics from a number of institutions. Disregarding the inconsistencies and difficulties in determining which countries people's ancestors came from, and acknowledging no other factors, genetic conclusions were drawn about individuals. Any examples of relatives having similar conditions were seized upon. These were then gathered into a study that statistically proved that certain racial and national types were criminalistic and amoral by their genetic nature. Such conclusions were presented to the U.S. Congress in 1922, and influenced immigration policy to limit non-Nordic quotas.[10] These immigration quotas would have tragic results when Jews fleeing Europe were denied admittance to the United States prior to World War II.

Immigrant groups didn't take kindly to these assertions, and eugenics was increasingly called a pseudo-science and criticized in the press for proposing to sterilize millions of Americans. By 1928, a review by the Carnegie Institute concluded that the voluminous family records of the ERO were little more than clutter, with very little scientific value. They attempted to persuade the organization to conduct genuine genetic research.[11]

It was not enough to document the superiority of the Nordic race. Vigorous steps were needed to protect society from defective germ plasm. Dr. John H Kellogg organized the first Race Betterment Conference in Battle Creek, Michigan, in 1914. Eugenic leader Harry Laughlin told the conference: "To purify the breeding stock of the race at all costs is the slogan of eugenics."[12]

For many years, the American Breeders Association included eugenics among its efforts. In 1911, they planned a campaign of "purging the blood of the American people of the handicapping and deteriorating influences of these anti-social classes."[13]

Groups identified included the feeble-minded, pauper class, inebriates, criminals of all descriptions including petty criminals and those jailed for non-payment of fines, epileptics, the insane, the constitutionally weak class (whoever *they* were), those predisposed to specific diseases, the deformed, and those with defective sense organs—the deaf, blind and mute. No distinction was made about degree of sensory defect. A definition of epilepsy was so broad it included those with migraine headaches and fainting spells. Negative eugenics would eventually embrace a number of solutions to protect society, including segregation, sterilization and euthanasia.[14]

In 1927, the Virginia eugenics law authorizing sterilization was tested. It involved the case of Carrie Buck, an eighteen-year-old feeble-minded girl. The U.S. Supreme Court upheld the state's right to involuntarily sterilize her, finding: "It is better for all the world, if instead of waiting to execute degenerate off-spring for crime, or to let them starve for their imbecility, society can prevent those who are manifestly unfit from continuing their kind. The principle that sustains compulsory vaccination is broad enough to cover cutting the fallopian tubes. Three generation of imbeciles are enough." [15]

This landmark Supreme Court case—which has never been overturned—bears the taint of an underlying misogyny.

The grandmother, Emma Buck, was committed as feeble-minded because of promiscuity. Immorality was widely accepted in court as proof of mental impairment. Her daughter, Carrie Buck, was placed in foster care and became pregnant when raped by her guardian's son. Carrie was then committed as mentally impaired, despite having been a good student, because she was immoral.[16]

Vivian Buck, the third generation, was examined when she was only seven months old by a social worker. When asked in court whether the baby was normal, the social worker replied, "There is a look about it that is not quite normal, but just what it is, I can't tell."[17]

Thus, the Supreme Court ruling that supported many state's adoption of sterilization laws was based not on three generations of imbeciles, but the mistreatment of three generations of women. The first was condemned for her sexuality, the second was blamed for being a victim, and the third labeled as the result of a ludicrous examination. This decision has to rank as one of the Supreme Court's worst, both because it had no basis in fact, and because of the harm that resulted from it.

Euthanasia, or the painless killing of the unfit, was discussed in England around the turn of the twentieth century. Lethal chambers had been employed there for some time to gas unwanted dogs. George Bernard Shaw was one of the eugenicists advocating putting people who needed someone to look after them out of existence.

The use of lethal chambers was discussed in American eugenic circles by 1910. A widespread debate erupted in the newspapers in 1915 after Dr. Haiselden, a Chicago physician, withheld medical care from a deformed newborn. An inquest upheld his right to do so. The doctor was quoted as saying he acted in accordance with eugenic principles. He justified his actions in part by pointing out that Illinois's institutions for the feeble-minded had death rates as high as twelve percent per year and were practicing passive euthanasia. He went on the lecture circuit, and played the part of a doctor in a Hollywood movie centered around a plot about allowing a defective newborn to die.[18]

Alexis Carrel, a Nobel Prize winning physician, provided an efficient answer, in 1935, for ridding society of gangsters and lunatics. He suggested that they be humanely and economically disposed of in small euthanisic institutions supplied with proper gases.[19]

Conflict eventually developed between negative eugenics, which stressed prevention of procreation by undesirables, and the growing scientific field of genetics. *The New York Times*, which had supported eugenic principles, by 1932 commented that eugenics had become a disguise for race prejudice and snobbery.[20]

NOTES

1. Christine Rosen. *Preaching Eugenics*, Oxford University Press, 2004, pp. 28-30.
2. *Preaching Eugenics*, p. 107.
3. American Eugenics Society, *A Eugenics Catechism*, ca. 1927.
4. Luta Kaelber. *Eugenics: Compulsory Sterilization in 50 American States*, University of Vermont, 2009, online.
5. Edwin Black. *War Against the Weak, Four Walls Eight Windows*, New York, 2003, p. 57.
6. *War Against the Weak*, p. 99.
7. Eugenics brochure, circa 1930, Dight papers.
8. *War Against the Weak*, p.81.
9. *ibid*, p. 46.
10. *ibid*, p. 191.
11. *ibid*, p. 388.
12. *ibid*, p. 88.
13. *ibid*, p. 32.
14. *ibid*.
15. *biid*, p. 121.
16. Ordover, Nancy. *American Eugenics: Race, Queer Anatomy and the Science of Nationalism*. University of Minnesota Press, 2003, p. 135.
17. *War Against the Weak*, p. 115.
18. *ibid*, p. 257.
19. *Mad in America*, p. 66.
20. *Preaching Eugenics*, p. 166.

Chapter Seven
Eugenics in Minnesota

THE EUGENICS MOVEMENT IN MINNESOTA did not focus on race. Instead, it concerned itself with preventing reproduction by defectives. In 1901, the first law in Minnesota was passed codifying eugenic principals. No man or woman under the age of forty-five who was epileptic, feeble-minded or insane could marry. Anyone issuing them a marriage license or performing a marriage ceremony was subject to a $1,000 fine and/or three years in prison.[1]

The eugeincs movement in Minnesota received a strong scientific base through genetic studies carried out at the Faribault School for Feeble-minded. The superintendent and a research assistant studied family histories of inmates beginning in 1911. A part of those studies were published in a book, *Dwellers in the Vale of Siddem: A True Story of the Social Aspect of Feeble-Mindedness.*

Inmates' relatives were interviewed as well as others in the community who knew the families. The first paragraph of the introduction states that, "These studies revealed an appalling amount of mental deficiency in particular districts of the state." One area was found to have such high numbers of "feeble-minded and degenerate people" that results from that county formed the basis of the book. Although not named, the county was said to be adjacent to the Mississippi River, with caves and valleys. A letter taped into a copy of the book in the Minnesota Historical Society library from a social worker in Lake City states that the survey was conducted in that area.

Charts of descendants from eight families were developed through four generations, totaling sixteen hundred individuals. Each individual was placed in a category including: normal, feeble-minded, epileptic, insane, sexually immoral, chriminalistic, alcoholic, tuberculosis, paralyzed, migrainous, nervous and unclassified.

Classifications overlapped, and placement wasn't always certain. Merrill Rogers, the author, wrote, "Often we are not satisfied to mark the individual feeble-minded and yet his reactions are such that he cannot be considered normal. In all such cases where there is any doubt about the classification the case has been considered doubtful and counted among the unclassified."[2] The majority of individuals fell into this classification.

The book's theme linked feeble-mindedness to heredity. The proof offered was the large number of deficient people living in a particular area of the state who were related to Faribault inmates. While only 199 of the sixteen hundred studied—twelve and a half percent—were placed in the feeble-minded category, heredity was said to be the cause of sixty-five percent of feeble-mindedness. Readers are presented with a confusing connection. Was it demonstrated that many feeble-minded people had feeble-minded ancestors? Or that the majority of the people living in the Vale of Siddem were defective?

To draw an analogy, it's one thing to say that the primary reason baked chicken is too dry is that it's cooked to long, and another thing altogether to say that all baked chicken is overcooked. One links cause and effect, the other speaks to frequency. *Dwellers in the Vale of Siddem* mixes the two so thoroughly that even a sophisticated reader is left with the impression that feeble-mindedness was both widespread and caused by heredity.

The high incidence of deficiency was due in part to a very broad definition of feeble-mindedness. In addition to mental tests, individuals had to pass a "social test" to be considered normal. This meant demonstrating the ability to maintain their existence independent of external support. There were those subjects as well who had properly developed intellectual faculties but lacked self-control, and were, thus, moral defectives. By the time anyone who'd had sex outside of marriage, needed assistance, committed a crime, had seizures or migraines and was nervous or drank too much was classified as defective, the majority of many populations could well have been included.

The beginning of the book included a discussion of Mendel's laws of genetics. Just like peas, the author argued that people could carry recessive genes, transmitting the possibility of feeble-mindedness down through the generations. Since someone who was normal to all outward appearances could be carrying a recessive defective gene, there was a significant chance that feeble-mindedness was flowing beneath the surface of typical society. This in turn was said to "give rise to a dull low level of intelligence in normals to whom the defect is transmitted in minor degree."[3]

Thus, the dwellers in the Vale of Siddem were said to have produced, "Moral obliquity, pauperism and vice, and the deadening social burden of deficiency and dementia . . ."[4] Given that such communities existed in the state, and their effects spread so perniciously, the dangers of unrestrained breeding had been clearly demonstrated in Minnesota by leading experts in the field.

The Reverend S.W. Dickinson of St. Paul advocated sterilization in a paper presented to Idaho Superintendents and reprinted in 1915. He wrote,

> Medical science considers feeble-mindedness, insanity, habitual criminality and like disorders as physical and mental diseases, capable of being transmitted in procreation. Sterilization cuts off the lines of descent only of such persons demonstrated to be unable to understand or morally able to control themselves, to prevent the continuance of their moral traits. Such persons, proven to be potential parents with undesirable hereditary potentialities and not likely to be governed by the highest moral purpose, should be humanely sterilized prior to their release, if now in institutions. Recent investigations have demonstrated that feeble-minded women are twice as prolific as the normal woman. Dr. Goddard has also found that the heredity of feeble-mindedness for the most part comes from the feeble-minded mother. While there can be no doubt that defectives, rapists and degenerates should be restrained from procreation, at present we would not include in the sterilization law moderate drunkard, vagrants and the like.
>
> As it is now in Minnesota, we cannot go into a family where there is a feeble-minded young woman, for

instance, and say to these parents: "This child of yours is defective and must be taken to an institution." If they so will, they can keep it at home all its life. The same is true of epileptics. Of course such a person is a menace to society. This class is far more prevalent than is generally supposed and cannot be dealt with until they commit some offense that makes them apprehensible.[5]

These early themes of linking immorality to feeble-mindedness, that women were primarily responsible, and the desire for doctors to search out defectives throughout society would reverberate in Minnesota eugenics.

Dr. Charles Dight, an eccentric Minneapolis doctor who dedicated his life to the betterment of mankind, was a socialist who believed strongly in sterilizing those with defective genes. While socialism and sterilization don't fit together within the present political lexicon, they were both efforts for the betterment of mankind. In 1923, he organized the Minnesota Eugenics Society and began a legislative crusade for a sterilization law. Founders included two University of Minnesota professors and a member of the Minneapolis Public Schools guidance department.[6]

Dr. Dight wrote over 300 letters to the editor and several pamphlets.[7] The vast majority of his writings speak of improving the human race by limiting the reproduction of the unfit. Behind that concern was an underlying racism, revealed in a paragraph from his pamphlet *Human Thoroughbreds: Why Not?* In this pamphlet, he wrote:

> At this time a situation is threatened where mental inferiority will dominate throughout the whole of the United States. War tests which have shown an unexpectedly low inborn mental ability among the American people indicate this. It is due in part to the great influx into this country of the mentally inferior of Europe and to their rapid reproduction. This has greatly lowered the average of American citizenship. We will **never recover from it except by the use of eugenic measures.** [Bold type in the original] The ad-

mission of undesirable immigrants, and the earlier impor-
tation of negroes as slaves have been the two great errors
committed by this republic—both of them for private profit
making. The results are here and the long period of national
repentance for these mistakes is at hand.[8]

The pamphlet, published in 1922, established—for those who were
paying close attention—Dr. Dight's racist views. He did not attempt to
promulgate racist policies, focusing instead on limiting the number of undesirables. He defined the problem as, "The socially unfit people in the
United States, including the hopelessly insane, the seriously epileptic, the
mentally subnormal and feeble-minded, those lacking altruism or who are
strongly inclined to some form of unsocial behavior are increasing at an
alarming rate."[6] Perhaps it was his socialist roots that led him to include those
who weren't altruistic. "Unsocial behavior" was in the eye of the beholder,
as shown by an examination of what happened to mothers of illegitimate
children.

An example of the rationale behind support for the sterilization law is
contained in a letter sent to probate judges by the Eugenics Society. The letter writers state that, "In a town within 18 miles of Minneapolis a feeble-
minded man and woman married and had seven feeble-minded children.
They were known as the 'family of nine fools.' Their descendants now number about 200 members none of whom are sound mentally. Similar cases
appear all over the country. Feeble-mindedness is hereditary and incurable."[9]
The Eugenics Society mailed letters to every legislator extolling the benefits
to society of sterilization.

Opposition to the Minnesota sterilization bill included concerns about
too much police power being given to doctors and the intrusion into family
life. The Catholic Church was firmly opposed to any method of birth control,
including sterilization.

Prominent supporters of the eugenics bill included Dr. Charles Mayo,
who wrote to the State Board of Control, "I think this bill is a good one and
if carried out under full restriction will greatly reduce in the future the number of our mentally unfit citizens."[10]

District Court Judge Guilford, another supporter, said, "It is a distinct step in the right direction." The former mayor of Minneapolis was quoted as saying, "To allow morons, epileptics, insane and feeble-minded to perpetuate their physical, intellectual and moral infirmities is a crime. There is a higher law than that of the individual. It is the well-being of society, and on one has the right to transmit to future generations infirmities that are vitally injurious to the race."[11]

The law easily passed the 1925 legislature, allowing for the sterilization of anyone committed as feeble-minded and insane individuals who had been institutionalized for at least six months. It required the consent of a spouse or guardian. [12]

Dr. Dight spent the rest of his life attempting unsuccessfully to get the law expanded to include mental defectives who weren't in institutions.

The American Eugenics Society began a eugenics sermon contest in 1926. On Mother's Day, the Reverend Phillips Osgood of St. Mark's Episcopal Church in Minneapolis delivered what would be the winning entry. Entitled "The Refiner's Fire," it called for improving the human race by enacting compulsory sterilization legislation. Rev. Osgood was a friend of Dr. Dight and joined him in his lobbying efforts.[13]

A 1926 pamphlet by the Minnesota Eugenics Society states that, "The unfit are multiplying rapidly, the more fit slowly. Average mentality is therefore being lowered and race degeneracy seems to be taking place." The pamphlet lists Eugenics Council members, including John P. Brown, executive secretary United Charities; Frederick Eliot, minister of Unity Church in St Paul; and E.P. Lyon, dean of the University of Minnesota Medical School, among many others.[14]

One suggested bill would have enabled the University of Minnesota to determine who should be sterilized. The dean of the university's medical school rejected that suggestion.[15] Catholics, on the other hand, introduced bills repeatedly to repeal the law.[16]

The Eugenics Society employed Mr. A.F. Lockhart to solicit donations. He kept detailed daily field notes in the fall of 1926. From these notes, we can see that donors included J.S. Pillsbury, J.A. Munson (of the Munsingwear Company), the secretary of the Retailer's Association, the county treasurer and Sheriff Earle Brown, a judge, the president of the Hennepin County medical association, several Episcopalian ministers and many doctors and lawyers, several of whom were noted to be Jewish. The one group he was not successful with was Catholics. His frustration with Catholics can be seen in his note of November 24, 1926: "Called on Dr. A.E. Anderson, but he was crabby and said he was not interested. I was told later on in the day that he is a Catholic convert, which is a gentle way of saying that his brain has atrophied." [17]

In an effort to recognize superior genetic qualities, the Minnesota Eugenics Society presented Charles Lindberg with a bronze plaque lauding his good heredity during a visit to Minneapolis on August 1, 1927.[18]

It can be seen that the eugenics movement had broad support in Minnesota. Leaders of business, medicine, government, and law agreed that sterilization of the unfit would benefit society. Even charities and churches felt that authority should be expanded to include those outside institutions. Dr. Dight was not some aberrant hatemonger, but the most visible spokesman for views held by many prominent citizens.

By 1930, the Minnesota Eugenics Society had faded away.[19]

Dr. Dight continued writing letters to newspaper editors extolling his beliefs. In Germany, Hitler instituted the Law for the Prevention of Defective Progeny on July 14, 1933. This was the first Nazi eugenic law. It called for the forced sterilization of 400,000 people with schizophrenia, manic depression, Huntington's chorea, epilepsy, hereditary body deformities, deafness and blindness.[20]

Two weeks later, Dr. Dight submitted the following letter to the *Minneapolis Journal*:

> The report persistently comes from Berlin that congenital feeble-mindedness, insanity, epilepsy, and some other serious conditions that are inheritable are to be stamped out among the German people. Adolf Hitler is having broad and scientific plans formed for this. If carried out effectively, it will make him the leader in the greatest national movement for human betterment the world has ever seen. The world's

two great needs are co-operation in industry for social good
and biological race betterment through eugenics."[21]

He followed up the next month by enclosing a copy of his letter to the
editor in a note to Adolf Hitler with the following remarks:

> Honorable Chancellor; I inclose [sic] a clipping from the
> *Minneapolis Journal* of Minnesota, United States of America,
> relating to, and praising your plan to stamp out mental in-
> feriority among the German people. I trust you will accept
> my sincere wish that your efforts along that line will be a
> great success and will advance the eugenics movement in
> other nations as well as in Germany.[22]

Hitler replied with a brief note translated as, "For the kindly extended attention towards me, I am expressing my cordial thanks. A. Hitler."[23]

Charles Dight died in 1938. The Nazis began killing handicapped children the following year, descending the final eugenic step in protecting society from defective genes.

Dr. Charles Dight's will bequeathed $75,000.00 to the University of
Minnesota to continue the promotion of eugenics. The purpose stated in
his will begins: "The entire yearly income thereafter shall be used wholly for
the following purpose:—To Promote Biological Race Betterment. . . ." This
would include education through classes and publications on heredity and
the principles of eugenics and promoting the application of eugenic measures. Eugenic societies were to be formed, and a place developed for con-
sultation and advice in promoting eugenic marriages. This would be done
by rating people as to their fitness to marry and reproduce.[24]

With the authorization of the Board of Regents, University President
Guy Stanton Ford named an advisory board that included six faculty members in June, 1941.[25, 26] The Dight Institute was to be housed in the Zoology
Department. A public announcement about the opening of the institute
called for donations of family histories. The minutes of the first meeting,
held on June 13, 1941, named Professor C.P. Oliver the director.[27]

From its beginning, the Dight Institute had close ties with the state hospital system. Dr. Royal Gray, the director of the mental health unit and in charge of all state hospitals, accepted a position with the Dight Institute's governing board on June 28, 1943.[28]

The first annual report of the Dight Institute, sent to the University of Minnesota president, lists a number of lectures given and research projects begun. These included the genetics of various dental conditions and breast cancer. Counseling was provided to individuals and through the Planned Parenthood League. Several bulletins were prepared for publication.[29]

The contrast between Dr. Dight's intention in his will—to promote race betterment—and the academic/professional tone of the annual reports is startling. From its beginning, the Dight Institute seemed to have two faces. To the academic community, it appeared to be at the forefront of the compassionate application of genetic science. Behind the scenes, however, some of its members remained strong advocates for eugenics.

The formation of a eugenics society was required by Dr. Dight's will and was still under consideration in 1945. Speaking about the relationship between the two organizations, the minutes of the Dight Institute's September 18, 1945, meeting include the following remarks from Professor Oliver:

> Other than its research and educational programs, the Institute should limit its eugenics program to consultation with persons who have immediate genetic and eugenic problems. This will include giving information about the probability of the occurrence of a specific trait in a person or his family and the genetic appraisal of the possibilities in their children where persons contemplate marriage or the production of children.[30]

This sounds much like contemporary genetic counseling. The odor attached to eugenics is obvious in the next quote from the minutes:

> Because of the erroneous conception the general public has about eugenics, an active program by the Institute at this

time [underlining in the original] to bring about legislation for the sterilization of groups or members of families, or an intensive program of propaganda of that sort, would cause the Institute to lose the public support and would make it very difficult for us to follow a research program in human genetics and eugenics. That part of a eugenics program can be accomplished better by another organization started for that purpose, such as a eugenics society, with which the Institute should cooperate."[31]

He makes his personal views clear by including a note saying, "I favor the use of legislation to bring about sterilization of individuals who have deleterious defects where it is established that sterilization can be effective in controlling the defect."[32]

Despite the earlier statement of purpose that sounds much like genetic counseling, he adds, "The Institute, acting as a research organization, should supply the information necessary to show the benefits to be derived from sterilization. It should help collect data which can be used by the Eugenics Society in its publicity."[33]

The Institute began a family history contest in 1943, with the Junior Minnesota Academy of Science. Only one submission was received in the first two years, but the National Science Teachers Association expressed interest.[34] Connections were developed with the national organization Birthright, which promoted voluntary sterilization. Uncomfortable with the controversy that developed between Birthright and the National Planned Parenthood League, the Dight Institute formed its own subsidiary in October 1945, called the Minnesota Human Genetics League, Inc., A Society for the Promotion of Population Research and the Improvement of Human Inheritance.[35]

Dr. Sheldon Reed took over as director of the Dight Institute in 1947. Courses were by this time offered in elementary and advanced genetics. Talks were given to adoption agencies, nurses, social welfare workers and churches. Funds were needed, and they received grants from the American Cancer Society and U.S. Department of Public Health.

Colonel Wycliffe Draper, a wealthy New Yorker, offered $100,000 for a "genetics project" to improve America by shipping African Americans back to Africa. The director didn't consider this to be a feasible research project for the Institute. Noting that the colonel didn't have an heir, Dr. Reed continued to maintain a friendly correspondence.[36] Apparently, while the Dight Institute wasn't carrying out an overtly racist program, it wasn't averse to soliciting a racist's money.

Harrry Laughlin, who had headed the ERO since its inception, had retired in 1939, and the Carnegie institute began dismantling the ERO. By 1944, Carnegie Institution executives became convinced that eugenics was a worthless nonscience based on shabby data.[37] Tainted by the revulsion generated when Hitler's genocide was revealed, the Carnegie Institute decided to get rid of the ERO records in 1947.

The Dight Institute, under Professor Sheldon Reed, requested the ERO's individual trait and family documents. The collection included 45,000 folders of pedigrees and over two million index cards. Reasons that Reed gave for requesting the material included the importance of the pedigrees. Another reason was the difficulty in obtaining pedigrees from Minnesotans because they frequently couldn't trace their ancestors past their grandparents before having to go to European sources. The third reason was sentimental—he felt Dr. Dight would have been pleased to get the collection.[38]

Carnegie supplied $1,000 to defray shipping costs, and the president of the University of Minnesota provided funds for ninety-six file drawers.[39] The eighteen tons of materials included data on families of individuals in the "Minnesota Institute for Defectives" at Faribault from 1911-1918.[40]

The Biennial Report of the Dight Institute for 1946-1948 ends by warmly thanking the president of the University, dean of the Graduate School and members of the Advisory Committee for their help and kindly interest in the development of the Dight Institute.

The University of Minnesota could be criticized for its support in acquiring such tainted and questionable data. The issue at the time wasn't completely clear, however. Reed defended the scientific value of the family histories, and he and his wife utilized the records to complete a study based on the records of the feeble-minded collected at the Faribault state school in 1911. They contacted over 80,000 people who were descendants of the original patients' grandparents. Their results reported that those people who they called retarded tended to have children with the same mental health issues.[41]

This might sound like a valid scientific use of the original data, perhaps not particularly noteworthy, but within the purview of science. That conclusion is weakened by the book's advocacy for voluntary sterilization. They claimed that a fifty-percent drop in the number of "retarded" people per generation could thus be attained.

Regents began discussing changing the name of the Dight Institute in 1985. State Representative Phillis Kahn introduced a bill in the legislature to ask the regents to consider a name change and report to the legislature in January of 1986. She said that because of his eugenics beliefs, honoring Dight was inappropriate.

A professor of genetics on the staff of the Dight Institute disagreed, saying, "The word eugenics at that time was the equivalent of human genetics. It has been used in a variety of ways, some of which we reject." He argued that Dight's writing and views should be separated from his bequest and the institute, which studied genetically-linked behavior disorders and diseases. One regent said he had not been aware of Dight's background.[42]

The Dight Institute didn't close its doors until the 1990s.[43]

NOTES

1. "A Review of the Laws," p. 3.
2. Rogers, Merrill. *Dwellers in the Vale of Siddem*, Gorham Press, Boston, 1919.
3. *ibid.*
4. *ibid.*
5. Dickinson, S.W. *Sterilization of the Habitual Criminal, epileptic, Insane and Feeble-minded—Is it Feasible?*, 1915.
6. Dight papers, correspondence, April 1925.
7. Temple, W. *History of the Early Stages of the Organized Eugenics Movement for Human Betterment in Minnesota*, Minneapolis, 1935, p. 7.
8. Dight, Charles F. *Human Thoroughbreds: Why Not?.* 1922.
9. *ibid.*
10. Meeting of the Executive Committee of the Minnesota Eugenics Society, March 1926.

11. Dight papers, correspondence, January 26, 1925.
12. Meeting of the Executive Committee of the Minnesota Eugenics Society, March 1926.
13. Gary Phelps. "The Eugenics Crusade of Charles Fremont Dight," *Minnesota History*, Fall 1984, p. 103.
14. *Preaching Eugenics*, p. 3, 124.
15. "Relating to MN Eugenics Society," circa 1926.
16. Dight papers, correspondence, November 15, 1926.
17. Sheldon Reed correspondence, Dight Institute, January 16, 1951, University of Minnesota archive.
18. Dight Papers, Field Notes.
19. Temple, W. *History of the Early Stages of the Organized Eugenics Movement for Human Betterment in Minnesota*, Minneapolis, 1935, p. 7.
20. Dight Institute, Bulletin number 1, 1943, University of Minnesota Archives.
21. *War Against the Weak*, p. 299.
22. Dight papers, scrapbook.
23. *ibid.*
24. *ibid.*
25. Public Welfare Dept, C.F. Dight will, March 1927.
26. Public Welfare Dept, Letter, June 10, 1941.
27. Letter Guy Ford to Dean Blegen June 10, 1941. Public Welfare, Dight Institute.
28. Public Welfare Department, Committee meeting minutes, June 13, 1941.
29. Public Welfare Deppartment, Letter to Dr. W. C. Coffey .
30. *Annual Report of the Dight Institute July 1, 1942 to June 30, 1943*. Public Welfare Dight Institute.
31. Public Welfare Department, Minutes of September 18, 1945.
32. *ibid.*
33. *ibid.*
34. Public Welfare Department, Minutes of September 18, 1945.
35. Oliver, C.P. *Report to the Committee of the Dight Institute for the Year 1945-46*. Public Welfare, Dight Institute.
36. Public Welfare Department, Minutes, October 8 and 23, 1945.
37. Public Welfare Department, *Biennial Report of the Dight Institute 1946-48*.
38. *War Against the Weak*, p. 387.
39. Dight Institute, *Conversational Report for the Dight Committee*, University of Minnesota Archives.
40. Public Welfare Department, *Biennial report of the Dight Institute for 1946-48*.
41. University of Minnesota Faculty Senate Minutes #3, February 12, 2004, Appendix A, online.
42. Reed & Reed. *Mental Retardation: A Family Study*, W.B. Saunders Co., Philadelphia, 1965.
43. *Minnesota Daily*, May 2, 1985, p. 1.
44. *War Against the Weak*, p. 397.

CHAPTER EIGHT
EUGENICS AND MINNESOTA STATE HOSPITALS

THE INFLUENCE OF THE EUGENIC MOVEMENT in Minnesota is clearest in the sterilization laws. However, state hospitals served to carry out the other two facets of eugenics as well—segregation and euthanasia. In this section, we will outline segregation and the laws regarding it in Minnesota.

SEGREGATION

IN 1851, DURING THE FIRST MEETING of the territorial legislature of Minnesota, a law was passed granting custody to the judge of Probate Court of "idiots, lunatics and other persons of unsound mind, and of persons who, in consequence of habitual drunkenness or for any other cause are incapable of the proper care and management of their own property, all of whom are known in the statue as insane persons or habitual drunkards." [1]

The law of 1868 clarified the commitment process. Private patients were those sent to the hospital by relatives and financially maintained by them. The probate judge issued warrants only when a person found to be insane was destitute.

An insane person was defined in the 1868 law as "every idiot, noncompos, lunatic and distracted person." This definition would stay in effect until 1935. By 1877, it was decreed that patients in the state hospital should be examined twice a year. Those found to be "not insane, but idiotic or weakminded or harmlessly demented or imbeciles" could be returned to their home counties. They could stay in the institution if the county couldn't care for them. [2]

In 1907, District Court judges could send people under indictment but found to be insane, an idiot or imbecile to the state hospital until they recovered, at which time they would be returned to court.

The 1917 law repealed previous statutes regarding the insane and established a comprehensive body of law regarding commitment. Anyone could apply to receive treatment at a state institution. Once admitted as a voluntary patient, the superintendent could detain them if he felt it would be unsafe to release them. A commitment petition would have to be filed within three days of the patient's demand to leave.

Any relative or reputable citizen of the patient's county could petition to commit someone. The county attorney would act on behalf of the patient to protect his rights, and the court would issue a warrant for the sheriff to bring the patient to appear in court. Two licensed physicians and the judge would examine such person and determine their defectiveness. If the person was found to be an inebriate or insane, the judge could commit the person to a state hospital or private institution. If the individual had not committed a crime, a relative or friend could apply to take charge of discharged patients.[3] It was after this law was passed systematizing the commitment process that increasing patient numbers gradually overwhelmed the system.

The 1935 law made minor changes, including the statement that patients found to be dangerous to the public by the committing court could not be released without the court's permission.

Beginning in 1945, interpreters were required during commitment procedures involving deaf and dumb patients. Conditions regarding patients who had been released on bond were altered. The court was authorized to revoke releases and request county attorneys to bring action against bond holders.

A 1947 law made substantial changes. New definitions and terms were used, including "mentally ill person," "senile person," and "mentally deficient person." The terms under which superintendents could retain voluntary patients were expanded. Instead of a criterion that it would be unsafe to release them, now the criterion was whether it would not be in the best interest of the person, his family or the public.

The sheriff's authority to take individuals into custody was also expanded in 1947, the law stating that, "The order of the court may be executed on any day and at any time thereof, by the use of all necessary means, including the breaking open of any door, window, or other part of the building, vehicle, boat or other place in which the patient is located, and the imposition of necessary restraint upon the person of such patient." A former state hospital staff member reported that sheriffs sometimes misled patients about where they were being taken. Patients were often confused about why they had been picked up, and may have believed they were going to jail or a general hospital. When they were turned over to the state hospital, some patients concluded that staff were involved in a conspiracy with the sheriff.[4]

Any reputable person could petition the court to restore a patient to capacity. Committed patients could be discharged to the care of a reputable person—usually a relative. A bond to the state could be required. The superintendent could discharge patients on a provisional basis for twelve months. If they had not been readmitted, the discharge became absolute and the person was restored to capacity.[5]

Even with these changes, patients with psychopathic personalities could not be released without court permission.[6] Committed patients were considered incompetent to marry, sign checks or vote.[7]

These discharge provisions would seem to provide for a number of routes patients could be released from commitment. However, the eugenic shame of having a "defective" family member caused many families to shun their hospitalized relative. Even if families weren't able or willing to go to court for a restoration of capacity, and wouldn't agree to be responsible for the patient, superintendents could discharge patients. In most hospitals, this didn't often happen.

It seems perfectly logical to us that if a patient demonstrated self-control, adequate social skills and could perform complex tasks, they should be considered for discharge. In practice, there was little connection between patient's performance and their release.

Admissions and discharges varied between hospitals. Moose Lake, in 1948, often discharged voluntary patients after three to five months. Those who had admitted themselves apparently left when they wished, and some were released despite being unimproved. Most patients were committed and provisionally discharged. Most were noted to be "improved" or "recovered." A few were said on discharge to be "not insane." After being out one year, their status was changed to discharged.

One surprising case was the provisional discharge of a patient listed as a "psychopath with moral deficiency" who was discharged after four months. Another patient was discharged from escape. Apparently, things didn't always go as planned or expected.[8]

A pattern of twelve-month hospital stays would be longer than modern expectations, but not unthinkable. Rochester State Hospital noted, in 1946, that some of the patients admitted as senile were in fact depressed. After several months, they were able to be discharged.[9]

Rochester's discharge rate of other types of patients was much lower. Prior to the use of electroconvulsive therapy, or ECT, sixty-five percent of patients with involutional psychosis remained hospitalized permanently.[10]

Anoka housed patients who were considered chronic, and their rate of discharge was quite low. In 1948, Anoka discharged only forty-one people and had thirty-five returns out of 1,340 patients. It was a hospital that received hopeless patients from other hospitals, so a lower rate would be expected. Even if they'd all succeeded in staying out on provisional discharge, forty-one patients was only four percent of the population. As it turned out, that dwindled after the returns to only four-tenths of a percent. This is more in keeping with the long term eugenic philosophy of segregation. Once committed, patients stayed.[11]

NOTES

1. Public Welfare Department, *A Review of the Laws of Minnesota Relating to the Feeble-Minded*, unpublished report, 1946 p. 1.
2. *A Review of the Laws of Minnesota Relating to the Feeble-Minded*. Public Welfare— Bureau Feeble-minded, 1935.
3. Minnesota Revisor of Statutes, 1917, online.
4. Hahn, Ruth. *What Was it Like to Be a Mental Patient in the State Hospital before 1950?*, St. Peter Regional Treatment Center Archives, p. 5.
5. "Public Administration Service," September 1950, St. Peter SH Collection, Archives, MN State University, Mankato.
6. Minnesota Revisor of Statutes, 1947, online.
7. Erickson, Wm. *The Great Charity. St. Peter Regional Treatment Center*, 1991 p. 99.
8. Moose Lake State Hospital, Admission record.
9. Rochester State Hospital Annual & Biennial Report, 1946.
10. Rochester Biennial Report, 1952.
11. Anoka, Progress Report, 1950.

CHAPTER NINE
SEGREGATION AND THE FEEBLE-MINDED

As MENTIONED IN THE PREVIOUS CHAPTER, commitment laws for the feeble-minded changed in 1917. Admissions to and discharges from Faribault had been voluntary. Now, patients considered to be mentally defective could be committed by a judge after a petition by any responsible resident. They were committed to the Board of Control because Faribault was overcrowded.[1]

The definition of "feeble-minded" at this time was: "Any person who is so mentally defective as to be incapable of managing himself and his affairs, and to require supervision, control and care for his own or the public welfare." The petition of a relative or reputable resident of the county led to the examination by a judge and two physicians. An examination by a person skilled in mental diagnosis—who often came from Faribault—was required. The doctors weren't required when the person was obviously feeble-minded.[2]

Efforts to deal with the feeble-minded centered on 'social control'.[3] The legal interpretation used for commitments was whether the individual was capable of adjusting with safety to themselves and society. It was not enough to have a low IQ. It had to be shown that they could not function normally in society without supervision.[4]

The Department of Social Welfare used the following criteria:

> The condition of feeble-mindedness must be established and rests upon the determination of intellectual incompetence, and developmental arrest, which are superimposed upon social incompetence. All factors of intelligence, adjustment, emotional traits and habits are given due consideration before commitment in order to ascertain the social capacity of an individual.

Once committed, they remained a ward for the rest of their life.[5]

The term "social incompetence" may seem benign, but was broad enough to include immorality as an indicator of dysfunction. Primarily applied to women, unmarried pregnancies or having multiple sex partners was enough to bring a person to the attention of social workers for further testing to determine whether they were defectives.

Opinions on how to determine feeble-mindedness swung back and forth. Downplaying the role of an individual's history, a Ramsey County judge, in 1943, felt that psychometric measurements had developed to the point that they were more accurate than observations, even if conducted over a considerable period of time. This was particularly true when there was a history of feeble-mindedness in the family.[6] Thus, a low IQ score would be enough for a judge to commit someone even if they had been living an independent life.

Commenting on the predominant importance of IQ scores, the state director of the Division of Research said in a letter to a Minnesota assistant attorney general,

> Whether or not a person with an IQ below 75 should always be committed as feeble-minded, so that necessary guardianship will be guaranteed, rather than left to chance and the opinions and inclinations of relatives and friends, depends on the standards in citizenship we wish to live up to, and on the chances we wish to take in assuming that a given individual will live up to them, with or without help.[7]

Dr. Kuhlmann pioneered IQ testing for the feeble-minded with subjects at Faribault. He developed an IQ test that was widely used by state examiners. He also set a cutoff point for determining feeble-mindedness stating, "that any case of mental arrest with an intelligence of 74 or lower may under any circumstances be properly classified as feeble-minded."[8] Those in the range of seventy-five to eighty-four he considered borderline, and those with eighty-five or over were within the range of normal.

At this time, the Stanford-Binet IQ test was in wide use across the United States. Criteria levels for the Stanford set sixty-nine and below as defective, below seventy-nine as borderline and eighty and above as normal. Thus, Stanford criteria levels were five points lower.

In 1938-1939, a psychologist studied fifty-one inmates at Faribault who were in their late teens. He gave each of them both the Stanford-Binet and Kuhlmann IQ tests and compared the results. Subjects, on average, scored seven points higher on the Stanford.

The combination of lower cut-offs on the Stanford plus seven extra points meant that subjects with near-average IQs were found to be above the defective cut-off on the Stanford, but below it on the Kuhlman. This led the examiner to conclude that "... the upper psychometric limit for mental deficiency should be placed at a lower point on the Kuhlmann scale."[9]

The record of those sterilized and segregated includes many who were married, found later not to be feeble-minded, and were successfully employed after release. This is not surprising, given that the test the state was using produced false positives for people with slightly below average intellectual ability. The state's sterilization focused on the "high grade" feeble-minded—the very people the state's test falsely labeled. They were not—and had never been—cognitively impaired. The extreme overcrowding at Faribault could have been relieved and thousands not stigmatized, incarcerated or sterilized if the IQ tests the State Research Bureau used had more accurately reflected those individual's abilities. It's impossible to know, but it is likely that the majority of the people sterilized in Minnesota had IQs within the normal range.

Not only the tests were invalid, but the conceptual basis of testing many of the subjects was flawed. The Kulhmann Test required teenage subjects to read and complete math problems. Testing someone's knowledge assumes that they are skilled in using the English language, have been exposed to mainstream culture and received an adequate education. None of these was a given in 1920s and 1930s Minnesota, filled as it was with immigrants and the rural poor.

The limits of IQ testing—stretched to the absurd—occurred with a Hispanic woman in the 1940s. Neighbors of Mrs. "T" contacted the Division of Social Welfare and said they were considering hiring a lawyer to get her out of Faribault. The children of Mr. and Mrs. T had been removed because of poor home conditions. Mrs. T was said to have had no schooling, and her parents never learned English. The director of Public Institutions wrote to the Faribault Superintendent, "When one looks at the record and sees she was married at 16 and has had a baby almost at the rate of one a year since then it would seem that even a person of rather high intelligence might have been unable to keep a clean home and care for the children. . . . it seems that it may be doubtful whether she is truly a feeble-minded person."[10]

What the director of the state institutions failed to mention were the factors that having come from an English as a second language background and having had no education might contribute to invalidating an IQ test.

The feeble-minded were committed to the guardianship of the director of the State Division of Social Welfare. Guardianship extended indefinitely through life.[11] Individuals wanting to be restored to capacity had to show that the original adjudication of feeble-mindedness was erroneous and that they were now competent to take care of themselves.

A case at the Minnesota Supreme Court in 1944 produced opinions about criteria and testing used to determine feeble-mindedness. Two friends of "R.M." wanted her restored to capacity and released from Faribault so she could return home and care for her children. The court ruled:

> Our statutes do not define "feeble-mindedness," nor has this court announced any hard and fast tests for determining the existence *vel non* of such condition. Neither have we found a comprehensive definition of the term in the decisions of other courts.
>
> To which we add, as applicable to the case here on appeal, that inadequate social adjustment at one time is not conclusive that such maladjustment will continue indefinitely. Hence, feeble-mindedness, viewed from a sociolegal rather than a purely medical standpoint, is not necessarily a "permanent' and "incurable" condition, as was stated by the trial court in its memorandum.
>
> The statement frequently made that all persons with IQs below 70 are feeble-minded is not justified, either

from the scientific or a practical point of view. Intelligence is made up of too many factors to permit of such a dogmatic statement.

There are no means at present available for testing to a certainty the condition of feeble-mindedness in that large percentage of cases whose intellectual level is within the range where it may partially but not wholly condition successful adjustment. While psychological tests are convenient tools for indicating mental retardation, test results alone should ordinarily not be considered sufficient, much less conclusive, except at the lower levels.[12]

It's significant that feeble-mindedness had not been clearly defined as late as 1944. New Deal programs led Governor Olson to designate the Board of Control to administer all forms of public assistance in the early 1930s. County welfare boards with greater financial and investigative powers replaced the largely voluntary child welfare boards. Some county boards ordered IQ tests for parents and families found to be living in deplorable conditions and had entire families committed as feeble-minded. Counties had a financial incentive to carry out testing because the state took on some financial responsibility for those deemed feeble-minded.

Later, some of those caught up in this process turned out not to be feeble-minded, because tests and decisions had been made too hurriedly, according to Mildred Thomson, who directed state guardianship. If they had been institutionalized, state officials couldn't end the guardianship that had been imposed by the probate court.[13]

By 1944, more than 10,000 people had been committed in Minnesota for life using an imprecise definition. The determination of feeble-mindedness took on added significance when it became the first step in the process of sterilizations.

As a result of these lifetime commitments, overcrowding was a chronic problem at Faribault. Early on, the Children's Bureau of the State Board of Control advocated, in 1918, for limiting the number of inmates at Faribault., saying that, "There should be room for low-grade helpless idiots and for higher-grade defective children in need of training in the manual arts, and the able-bodied, feeble-minded patients should grub the land and till the soil in colonies of modest structure on undeveloped state lands in northern Minnesota."[14] Personally, I shudder to think of groups of feeble-minded patients having to hack out a habitation for themselves in the forests of northern Minnesota.

A waiting list developed of over a thousand committed feeble-minded patients. The Director of Public Institutions asked the county poor farms throughout the state to consider boarding some of the older inmates from Faribault. The rationale given was that they were over fifty years of age and were no longer able to give birth.[15] Thus, they no longer had to be segregated in the closely monitored confines of Faribault State Hospital.

The Minnesota Medical Association was asked to conduct a survey of Faribault and investigate allegations of maltreatment. They completed their meetings and inspections and issued a report in April 1947. They felt the institution was being run as well as could be expected under the circumstances, but had a number of criticisms.

There were 500 more patients than would be acceptable under national standards. Some buildings were obsolete, poorly equipped and unsafe. The main kitchen was inadequately equipped and could produce only steamed or boiled food three hours before it was served, and nine and a half cents was being spent per meal per person. In one building, one-third of the patients were in restraints because there were too few staff to allow them to move about without assistance. A dozen children were tied to toilets. Younger children were inadequately clothed. They urged the legislature to provide more money for food, salaries and equipment.[16]

As an occupational therapist, it is particularly galling to me that instead of providing the braces, walkers, wheelchairs and therapy that would have allowed children to move about, they were restrained.

NOTES

1. *Report of the Children's Bureau State Board of Control*, 1918, pp. 7-9.
2. *A Review of the Laws of Minnesota Relating to the Feeble-Minded*. Public Welfare— Bureau Feeble-minded, 1935.

3. Letter Mildred Thompson to Judge G Loevinger, March 15, 1944, Faribault Superintendent subject files—letters.
4. Letter Judge Loevinger to Mildred Thomson, March 13, 1944, Faribault Superintendent subject files—letters.
5. History of the Sterilization of the Feeble-Minded, Faribault Superintendent Correspondence, Sterilization file, ca 1940.
6. Ramsey County District Court # 245713, February 18, 1943, Faribault Superintendent subject files—letters.
7. Letter, Director Division of Research to Roy Frank, January 8, 1934, Public Welfare—psychological services.
8. Kuhlmann, F. A. *Handbook of Mental Tests*. Warwick & York, 1932.
9. Carlton, T. A. *Comparison of the Revised Stanford-Binet, Form L, with the Kuhlmann Tests of Mental Development*. J Genetic Psychology, 1942, pp. 61, 47-54, Faribault Published Reports .
10. Letter, Carl Swenson to E. Engberg, November 1, 1946, Public Welfare Psychological Services.
11. Letter E. Enberg, Superintendent to J Pero, Director Social Service ,Utah, May 26, 1941, Faribault Superintendent subject files, sterilization.
12. State of Minnesota Supreme Court, Opinion and Syllabus, March 3, 1944.
13. Ladd-Taylor, Molly. "Eugenics and Social Welfare in New Deal Minnesota." In *A Century of Eugenics in America*, Paul Lombardo Ed., Indiana University Press, 2011.
14. *Report of the Children's Bureau State Board of Control*, 1918 pp. 7-9.
15. Letter, Carl Swanson, October 30, 1942, Faribault State School and Hospital correspondence.
16. *A Report by the Special Committee Appointed by the Council of the Minnesota State Medical Association at the Request of Governor Edward Thye*, April 16, 1947. Governor Youngdahl Records, Public Institutions.

CHAPTER TEN
STERILIZATION

THE EUGENICS MOVEMENT ADVOCATED STERILIZATION of those deemed unfit to procreate. In a paper read at a conference for State Superintendents in Boise Idaho in 1915, Reverend S.W. Dickinson from St. Paul advocated for sterilization, saying, "The greatest criminal danger connected with the criminal class, the feeble-minded, the insane and the rapist is their abnormal desire for procreating. The exercise of that power is a moral, and ought to be a legal, crime. The degenerate have a right to live, but they have no right to curse their offspring. Prevention is a social and Christian duty."[1]

After applauding states where authority had been given to sterilize those in institutions, he went on to advocate including "pronounced cases of the same class outside." This would be done by creating boards with powers to examine those suspected of being defective or degenerate. County or town officers, or any reputable citizen could petition to have someone examined. They would then be segregated and sterilized. The Minnesota Eugenic Society's bill closely followed these proposals.[2] This would have amounted to sterilizing about ten percent of the state's population.[3] The Minnesota State Board of Control, which would have had the responsibility of carrying out these proposals, objected that it was unprepared to do so.

In 1925, a more limited Minnesota sterilization passed eighty-six to thirty-seven in the house and forty to four in the Senate.[4] It authorized sterilization by tubectomy or vasectomy for those committed as feeble-minded or who had been committed as insane and institutionalized for at least six months, with the consent of their spouse or nearest relative[5]

Draconian as this may seem, some continued to call for widening the authority to include anyone in the population deemed unfit. A professor of anthropology at the University of Minnesota stated, "To be effective all subnormals should be sterilized whether or not they approve, and none such should be turned loose to destroy the character of other persons by sexual contacts."[6] Surrounding states did just that. Michigan, Iowa, North Dakota, and South Dakota law authorized the compulsory sterilization of those outside institutions.

The phrase "those who had been committed as feeble-minded" is assumed by many to mean that candidates for sterilization were individuals who had been sent to Faribault because they required institutional care, perhaps many years prior to their surgery. This is not what happened in practice. The seemingly minor distinction between the six-month commitment required for insane patients prior to surgery and merely a commitment as feeble-minded meant that women were scooped up out of society and sent to Faribault to be sterilized. In the case of the feeble-minded, the wider eugenic objective of sterilizing defectives outside of institutions was pursued in Minnesota.

The first sterilizations were carried out on six adult feeble-minded females on January 8, 1926, at the Faribault State Hospital. Dr. George Eitel, a prominent Twin Cities surgeon, performed the operations. The occasion was momentous enough that Dr. Dight attended to witness the beginnings of this new and useful procedure. [7]

The Eugenic Society remained closely involved in the application of the law, suggesting procedures and paperwork. Frustrated with the slow implementation by the State Board of Control, a meeting was held in the governor's office in January 1926. Dr. List offered the services of the Minneapolis General Hospital to perform sterilizations, but members of the State Board of Control made no commitments.[8]

Sterilizations of the insane varied between hospitals. Between 1942 and 1950, Anoka, Cambridge, Hastings and Rochester reported no sterilizations. Moose Lake sterilized one female patient per year for three of those years. St. Peter sterilized one female patient over the course of three years, and a total of one male between 1942 and 1950. Over the course of three years, Fergus Falls sterilized six females and four males.[9]

While sterilizations of the insane were infrequent and haphazard, they were routine policy for the feeble-minded. Speaking of the group of people released under supervision, the Children's Bureau stated,

A general policy of the State Board of Control is to parole
an adult only after an operation for sterilization so that more
than half of this group are sterile. The intent of the marriage
law is to prevent the birth of children to feeble-minded parents, and if one party to the marriage is sterile then that couple will not become parents. Marriage where there will not
be children is an excellent adjustment for the high-grade
moron. Despite the law which says the feeble-minded shall
not marry, many sterilized wards have done so, and as a
whole have proved the truth of the above statement.[10]

The rationale behind sterilizing the feeble-minded was quite convoluted. One reason given was that they were unfit to be parents. This was reflected in the frequent comments that a candidate for sterilization was unable
to care for her children.

The prevention of inherited feeble-mindedness was also frequently
cited. A 1930 survey of members of the American Association for the Study
of the Feeble-Minded downplayed genetic factors as a rationale for sterilization. This scientific opinion was issued before the era of most of Minnesota's sterilizations. The often-asserted eugenic position that sterilization
would improve humanity had lost much of its scientific underpinnings
shortly after the law permitting them in Minnesota had passed. While this
was becoming clear to academics, in the public's mind eugenics continued
to be seen as scientific fact.

It may have become obvious that all of humanity couldn't be altered,
but the units of government involved in providing care to the feeble-minded
could make sure that certain individuals didn't reproduce. Having given
birth to a defective child provided the reason for some sterilizations, as did
having a large family on welfare.

The major rationale remaining for sterilizations among the feeble-
minded in Minnesota appeared to be the "social capacity" of individuals.
This placed less emphasis on genetic science, instead focusing more on
whether individuals were self-supporting or were a drag on society. It was
believed that if they were not living up to expected norms, they should not

be allowed to have children. One of these norms was that females would have sex only if married. Immorality was thus linked to being morally defective. Anyone needing public assistance also lacked social capacity, and low IQ scores confirmed these conditions.

There were 7,278 epileptic or feeble-minded individuals under commitment in Minnesota by 1940. Another 3,500 children were being educated in special classes throughout the state. This was contrasted to an estimated 100,000 feeble-minded persons in the state, based on a survey showing that four to five percent of the population was "... socially incompetent, with this incompetence due at least in part to defective intelligence. Consequently, adding the committed cases, those who are under supervision thru special classes in the schools, it appears that less than 10% of the feeble-minded in the state are receiving either institutional or extramural services."[11]

Since ninety percent of them didn't need assistance, it could have been concluded that the vast majority of so-called feeble-minded individuals were functioning well and independently in society. Instead it was said, "Thus we have under guardianship only a small fraction of the group which are actually or potentially parasites upon the social order to which they cannot contribute."[12] This harsh view reflects the mindset of professionals providing services to the feeble-minded and is in keeping with eugenic concerns.

After an individual's commitment as feeble-minded, the Faribault superintendent, a physician and psychologist, considered each case recommended for sterilization. The process for selecting those to be sterilized was as follows:

> Selection of individuals is made by the staff, and based on the evidence that the individual might be able to maintain himself in whole or in part under supervision. . . . The sterilization operation is not performed usually unless it is thought that the inmate will be suitable for parole; and parole of the female during the child bearing age, and of the male irrespective of age, does not occur ordinarily unless sterilized.[13]

Plans for supervision after release were reviewed as part of the pre-operation consideration process.

Beginning in 1926, the record of sterilizations at Faribault includes the dates when the following signatures were obtained for each patient: personal consent, consent of guardian, recommendation of the superintendent, examination authorized by Board of Control, the examiner, interviewed by Board of Control, operation authorized by Board of Control, operation, and discharged to whom.[14] Personal consents for the operation were obtained by the hospital social worker in a private interview, and inmates signed in the presence of two witnesses.[15]

This record of thorough approvals would seem to indicate that sterilizations in Minnesota were voluntary. Board of Control policy stated that inmates wouldn't be released unless sterilized. However, this wasn't made clear in discussions with guardians and patients when seeking consent for the operation, though the policy stated, "It is further emphasized that no pressure be brought to urge sterilization but that patients be allowed free choice of action with their realization that plans may be made more readily after sterilization has improved their chances of making an outside adjustment."[16]

We can't know what went on in those conversations, but hints appear that being willing to be sterilized was linked to release. A psychologist at Faribault sent the following in a letter to the Social Security Division in St. Paul: "As you may recall, it is the wish of the mother to have Annette released, and she told me she was willing to sign a consent to a sterilization operation if necessary."[17]

On the other side of this official sophistry were cases where an individual or guardian not only wanted the inmate out, but released to a particular setting. Placements depended on the inmate's functioning after recovering from the operation, and available openings:

> The director of the Division of Social Welfare requires that
> no bargain be made with any person, that if sterilization is
> agreed to, some specific plans will be made. No pressure
> may be brought to urge sterilization against the religious
> and moral convictions of the person whose consent is nec-

essary. However, it is conceded that plans may often be made more easily and satisfactorily following the operation. This may be stated tentatively, and plans outlined but is must be clearly stated that there is no assurance that the Superintendent of the School for the Feeble-Minded will approve of the operation.[18]

Candidates for sterilization came from a number of sources. Some were "high grade" males and females already in the Faribault institution. Parents brought children in, as reported in the 1928 Biennial Report, which stated,

> Several patients of very low-grade mentality were sterilized upon the request of the parents, not with the idea of their ever becoming self-supporting, but that they might be supervised at home, when the danger of complications had been eliminated. Everyone connected with the work feels that the law is operating very satisfactorily, but wishes its scope could be broadened.[19]

Later, patients also came from the State School at Owatonna.[20] Residents at Cambridge were also culled for parole candidates and transferred to Faribault.[21]

The policies and rules of the Division of Research in 1935 included testing girls committed to the Home School for Girls at Sauk Centre and women sent to the Reformatory at Shakopee, and all delinquents in court if mentality was in doubt.[22] The term "sex delinquent," if used today, would imply a young person who had committed a crime of rape or engaged in prostitution. In the first half of the twentieth century in Minnesota, it described a female who had sex outside of marriage.

The director of the Bureau of Research wrote to explain the difference in IQ scores between a University of Minnesota study and the survey conducted by the state Research Bureau. He felt that the two groups of female sex delinquents were not comparable, for one came from out-state, and one from the Twin Cities. He wrote,

> When your sex delinquents have had a mental test it means
> that they were brought in for a hearing in feeble-minded-
> ness, or were suspected of mental deficiency and given a
> mental test out of court. If they were sex delinquents with
> apparent normal intelligence they passed through the court
> without a mental test. In the Twin Cities any sex delinquent
> is more likely to be brought in for a mental test, irrespective
> of suspected mental deficiency.[23]

The case files from the Home School for Girls in Sauk Centre include many adolescents who were sent to the institution as "incorrigible" because they stayed out late and had multiple sex partners. Despite having committed no property or violent crimes, they were committed as delinquents until they were twenty-one.[24] While in Sauk Centre, they were given IQ tests. Those who scored low were sterilized before being released.[25]

However, women didn't have to be delinquent to get swept into the system. The Faribault admission records from the early 1930s includes many cases of women admitted and then discharged after less than a year. In one case, the record says a woman was "admitted for sterilization" and discharged after eight weeks. Reasons for admitting women for sterilization included having had a feeble-minded child, an illegitimate child, prostitution, using "considerable alcohol," immorality, ". . . a long history of sex life," and promiscuity.[26]

Pregnant women needing public assistance were identified as possibly feeble-minded by the Infant Welfare Society, visiting nurses and the social service departments of general and university hospitals.[27] Testing in maternity hospitals was conducted by the Research Bureau of the State Board of Control. In the fiscal year ending July 1942, testing was done for the Children's Protective Society, Children's Service, Children's Home Society, Jewish Welfare of St. Paul, Bureau of Child Welfare, Minnesota Training School, St. Paul Public Schools, Home School for Girls, Women's Reformatory, and M.S.R. Reformatory, among others.[28]

The Research Bureau of Minnesota's State Board of Control studied 344 unmarried mothers who were in Maternity Hospitals in 1925, and found that sixty-seven percent had below average IQs. From this, the Bureau recommended, "That every unmarried mother should be given a mental test as the first step in the effort to understand her as an individual. That girls found to be feeble-minded should be prevented, if possible, either by segregation, close supervision or sterilization from having more children."[29]

Pregnant women who had low IQs and received services through maternity hospitals were sent to court to be committed to Faribault. Shortly after the birth of their child they were sterilized. After a three-month nursing period required by the State Board of Control, the babies were removed from their mothers and returned to their home counties.[30]

What happened to the babies after they were sent back to the counties isn't in the Faribault record. The policy of maternity hospitals in the Twin Cities was to place all babies of unwed mothers with relatives or out for adoption or boarding, unless the woman planned to marry the father.[31]

From July 1939 to June 1940, fifty-four pregnant women were admitted to Faribault for confinement during their pregnancy. Of these, nineteen were married mothers, twenty-six were unmarried, six were married with an illegitimate child, two were widowed with an illegitimate child, and one was divorced with an illegitimate child. Of these fifty-four women, forty-four were released after three months. Ten were to remain indefinitely.[32]

The Minnesota Department of Social Security continued to advocate for committing pregnant women for confinement at Faribault, followed by sterilization, well into the 1940s. Mildred Thomson wrote, "Many of those for whom operations are to be approved would probably never have operations if they were not first there for confinement, and some of these are where they are most necessary. Of course, I should like to see sterilization operations performed also and I fully realize what your inadequate staff at the hospital means."[33]

The state sometimes overrode an individual's plans, completely altering their lives. The following letter from Mildred Thomson concerns a woman with a five-week-old baby.

October 25, 1930

My dear Dr. Murdoch:

> *(_____) is a girl who has been considered for entrance to Cambridge ... the Board of Control has agreed that she be sent to Faribault and she will bring her baby, born 9-13-30 with her.*
>
> *It was expected that she would be entered at Cambridge as soon as the baby had been weaned, but she is now planning to get married and it is thought that she should be immediately institutionalized. The baby is to be removed from the institution as soon as you think best.*
>
> *We will consider this girl for the space of one of the girls who has been operated on and who is to be paroled.*

Very truly yours,

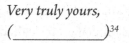

Even with the most benign possible scenario—that she was released immediately after being sterilized, was free to get married, and regained custody of her baby—this seems to be a gross interference in someone's life. She was not a criminal. Presumably, if she had been considered for admittance to Cambridge, she had epilepsy. This was enough for the state to decide that even though she would be complying with the social norm of raising a baby within a marriage, she couldn't be allowed to have more children.

There was a waiting list of over a thousand to get into Faribault. Three to five years typically elapsed between the time someone was committed as feeble-minded and their admission to Faribault.[35] This was not true for sterilization cases. Female delinquents and pregnant welfare patients were quickly admitted.[36]

Passing a pre-surgical physical was fairly easy. Commenting on the sterilization procedure, Dr. George Eitel—who regularly performed the operation—stated, "We have been able to do those with bad heart conditions and also those with pulmonary tuberculosis. So I do not feel there is really any contra-indication for this particular operation in itself."[37]

Severe seizures—unless they occurred shortly before the operation—weren't an impediment. Pre-surgical examinations were so cursory that in one case, the patient was found during the operation to be two months pregnant. The baby was born healthy, despite the completed operation.[38] In another case, when the patient was opened up, they found an ovarian cyst and such extensive adhesions that the operation couldn't be completed. They concluded that the patient had probably been sterile already.[39]

Little consideration was given to the recovery process when selecting candidates for the operation. Some incisions became infected, and one patient tore out her stitches. Several recoveries were lengthy, with patients spending over a year in the infirmary.[40]

The first surgeries weren't always successful in preventing pregnancies. Out of 440 of the first women sterilized by bilateral tubectomys, ten later got pregnant. Three of these women were later reoperated on by Dr. Eitel. He found that an irregular channel had re-established continuity so he modified the operation in 1933, and no more pregnancies occurred.[41]

While the official policy called for sterilizing only patients with established discharge plans, life wasn't always so clear-cut. The Children's Bureau reported the disposition of 157 females who had been sterilized by June, 1928. Of these, thirty-two were in club houses, seventeen were returned to their husbands, thirty-six were returned to their families, eighteen were other paroles, fourteen were returned to an institution after parole, four were discharged to marry, two were placed out of state, two died, eight were lost, and twenty-four were never paroled.[42]

Things happened, and patients became lost to the system, or their placement didn't work out and they had to be returned to the institution. The twenty-four who were never paroled are more difficult to understand. Were plans made for release that never worked out? Were they sterilized even though there were no plans to let them go? In at least one case, sterilization was considered so important that a family asked that a girl be sterilized even though she would have to remain institutionalized. They felt the operation would enable her to be come home for vacations.[43] You have to wonder what they thought that vacation would entail.

There has been some speculation about why so many more women than men were sterilized. In other states, this was not the case. Was this a case of Minnesota misogyny? Was it because men were making the decisions? In the latter case, however, men *weren't* making all the decisions. Mildred Thomson headed the Bureau for Feeble-Minded and Epileptics from 1924 to 1959. She supported and assisted in arranging for sterilizations well into the 1950s.

Some of the difference in sterilization rates was due to the relative ease of placing female inmates afterward. There were a number of "club houses" in the Twin Cities for feeble-minded women. These included the Harmon Club in Minneapolis, Lutheran Woman's Home in Minneapolis, the Minneapolis Club, the St. Paul club, the Lynnhurst Club, the Industrial Club, the Redwood County Home, the Park Avenue Club, and the YWCA. Residents worked in menial jobs, paying part of their salary for room and board.[44] Placements for men were more difficult to find, and were usually on farms.[45]

The records show a number of instances where the primary concern about the spread of defective progeny was placed on females. Several married women recommended for sterilization had husbands considered stupid or borderline, or who were in jail or neglected their family. Of the couples involved, it was the women who were selected for sterilization.[46]

In a case taken to the Minnesota Supreme Court, a married couple with ten children were on relief. Social workers became concerned about the dirty house and unkempt children and removed the eight children still at home. Welfare workers ". . . concluded that unrestricted fertility on the part of Mr. and Mrs. M was not consistent with their economic and social capacities." Both parents were found to be feeble-minded, but only the wife was sent to Faribault. There is no indication that either the lower court or Supreme Court asked why the wife was deprived of her liberty, but not the husband.[47]

Commenting on the composition of the waiting list of over 1,200 individuals to get into Faribault, the Children's Bureau reported that, "A large percentage of the higher-grade females in the group over eighteen years old, and some of those in the 13-18-year group, have been sexually delinquent, while many males in the same age groups show delinquencies of various types."[48] As we can see, concern about delinquency was focused on sexuality with females, but not with males.

A survey proposal noted that during child-bearing years, three times as many females than men were being given IQ tests. Two reasons were given. The first was that unmarried women were easier to find than unmarried fathers. The second reason ". . . is the deeply rooted conviction that the feeble-minded female is more responsible for feeble-minded children than is the feeble-minded male, and that therefore preventative measures are more important for the female. Of course, this cannot be so to any great extent for hereditary cases, if the Mendelian law is applicable to the feeble-minded."[49] Despite the acknowledgement within the Bureau that this prejudice had no scientific basis, a disproportionate number of women continued to be sterilized.

State-wide IQ testing of school children was proposed in the Bureau of Feeble-Minded in the early 1930s. Those scoring under seventy-five would be registered as feeble-minded and closely observed by county welfare boards. Commitment would only be done for special reasons.

A concern was expressed about whether sterilization would increase promiscuity. A fear of pregnancy was considered to be a restraining influence on sexual activity. A survey of 906 patients in 1939 who had been sterilized in Minnesota refuted this. The majority were said to have had sex only before their operation and none afterward. This same survey documents the differences in sexual activity before sterilization. Sixty percent of the females had been sexually active before they were sterilized, compared to thirty percent of the males.[50]

It would be tempting to thoroughly condemn the whole sterilization process. Inmates were given the choice of being sterilized as their only hope for being released. Unmarried mothers were caught in the system, labeled "delinquent" and strongly encouraged to be sterilized. If they'd been incarcerated as delinquents, it was a requirement to get out. Operations were done on medically fragile and pregnant patients.

Some parents, however—and patients—viewed sterilization as a beneficial method of birth control. A 1945 letter discussing possible candidates for sterilization repeatedly refers to the operation as providing "protection."

Used as a method of birth control, women were protected from becoming pregnant and for males, it protected the community.[51]

Up until 1957, the standard consent form signed by inmates included the statement, "I also give consent for the surgeon to correct any other surgical condition or disease that might be present within the abdomen."[52] While the abdominal cavity was open, surgeons routinely examined for abnormalities and performed necessary additional surgeries. Appendectomies and tumor removals were common. From the staff's viewpoint, this was another positive outcome of the sterilization procedure.

The picture gets more complicated when married people are added to the mix. The record of the first thousand sterilizations at Faribault includes a number of cases of women being released to their husbands, and a few of husbands being released to their wives.[53] Additionally, in a number of cases, women later married. It was noted that, "A considerable number of the commitments we make now are of parents with from one to a dozen children." The suggestion was made that these individuals be committed before they married and reproduced.[54]

All of the people discussed so far were found to be "defective" by a combination of mental and social tests. There was also a group of mentally normal women who underwent the procedure. Social workers persuaded women who had "... a large family, some of whom were mentally deficient" to be sterilized.[55] These would appear to be examples of genetic counseling, something that some prospective parents seek today. Experts at that time were divided on how direct the influence of heredity was on disabilities. The sterilization program was thus not a monolithic evil, but the result of a complex mix of motivations.

Some social workers and family members were concerned for the wellbeing of children, and some focused on independent lives for feeble-minded adults. Others were primarily concerned about limiting the births of defectives. It may have seemed very positive to be able to offer an inmate of Faribault a way to get out. In the eyes of those in the system, and society in general, sterilization was an expedient measure.

It's difficult to conceive of any justification for having pulled women out of the general population and into the system because of their sexual activity.

Some protections were in place for patients who were already in Faribault. A family member had to give permission and the approval of the individual to be sterilized was routinely sought. This was true of the cases of women delinquents transferred from Sauk Centre to Faribault to be sterilized.

It could be argued that none of these people could give a true informed consent. Their mental capacity was by definition diminished, and the only way they could get out was by agreeing to be sterilized. However, not even this thin pretext of seeking permission occurred when women were committed to be sterilized. The court ordered them in, they were sterilized and released.

While the state hospital system was complicit in this process, there were far bigger responsibilities. Social workers and community members identified these women. The court system—acting carefully as agents of state law—were a prime factor in determining that the women had no choice. Social workers and courts acted as agents of society, who were content to see societal sexual norms brutally enforced. There are those today who decry populist politicians who wage "class warfare." The sterilization record in Minnesota documents such a war, waged by the majority against the poor. The first step for most sterilization candidates was to come to the attention of a social worker. From there, a referral for testing would be made.

Policies published by the Public Welfare Department included the following:

> *WHOM TO REFER*
> *In general, individuals should be referred who present problems of personal or social adjustment in the understanding of which the case worker desires assistance. The following kinds of individuals are typical of those for whom the case worker and psychologist cooperatively may work out a helpful course of action: adults in need of vocational guidance, unmarried mothers when the worker is attempting rehabilitation, children showing a poor school adjustment, children with physical handicaps, dependent children for whom placement and school plans must be made, juvenile delinquents or pre-delinquents of interest to the*

probate court, and children failing to adjust in foster homes. A
common practice to be discouraged is to refer only those cases
suspected of mental deficiency.[56]

In other words, someone could be rich and retarded, rich and promiscuous, rich pregnant and single and not be sterilized. Or, someone could be on welfare and have too many children, poor and have a handicapped child, poor and have a dirty home, poor and turned in for promiscuity, poor and pregnant and they'd be sterilized.

Sterilizations declined in the state because they had to. The rate of sterilizations decreased drastically during the Second World War because of a shortage of surgical nurses. Males needed less post-operative care, and their rates didn't decline as much.

The successful placement of many people who were wards of the state into the military and industry during World War II helped bring about a change in attitude. The war provided many individuals who had been classified as feeble-minded opportunities to successfully live independent lives. Mildred Thomson, who had played a central role in arranging for sterilizations, said, "If they were able to show greater ability and better judgment than we had expected, perhaps we need not be so concerned about the possibility of their having offspring. Moreover, some of the knowledge of human genetics gained during these later years had ended the idea that mental deficiency was inherited as an entity." Displaying her continuing belief in the surgery, she went on, "Thus sterilization could be considered on a more selective basis."[57]

Mildred Thomson's newly enlightened attitude toward sterilization was based not on human rights, but economic utility. That's a limited and uncomfortable yardstick that few of us would like to see applied, for example, when examining the economic usefulness of those who are retired. She offered no apology, either, for having forged ahead and permanently diminished people's lives on the basis of flawed testing that said people were incapable who later proved they could live on their own.

By 1949, Minnesota had sterilized 79.1persons per 100,000 of the population. As high as this might seem, North Dakota's rate was 122.3.[58]

Advocacy of sterilization continued as late as 1950, when Dr. Clarence Gamble read a paper at the American Psychiatric Association annual meeting. He cited benefits to the potential parent who is spared the stress of child rearing, the child who may be raised in foster care, and the costs society avoids.[59]

By 1954, a total of 2,275 people had been sterilized in Minnesota— 286 insane females and 118 insane males; 1,478 feeble-minded females and 393 feeble-minded males.[60] Annual sterilization statistics had been collected for every institution by Birthright.[61]

Additional safeguards limiting sterilization were put in place in 1975. Final numbers of those sterilized cannot be determined, because sterilization is still permitted in Minnesota upon a court order.[62]

NOTES

1. "Sterilization of the Habitual Criminal," unpublished paper, S.W. Dickinson, St. Paul, 1915, p. 3.
2. Dight papers, correspondence, circa 1925.
3. Molly Ladd-Taylor. "Eugenic Sterilization in Minnesota," *Minnesota History*, summer 2005, p. 241.
4. Temple, W. *History of the Early Stages of the Organized Eugenics Movement for Human Betterment in Minnesota*, Minneapolis, 1935, p. 9.
5. "Review of Laws," p. 5.
6. *Eugenics Crusade*, p. 104.
7. Dight papers, "A Brief Account of the Early History of the Eugenics Movement in Minnesota."
8. *ibid.*
9. Human Betterment Foundation sterilization statistics, University of Minnesota Archives, Dight Institute.
10. *Biennial Report of the Children's Bureau*, June 30, 1936, p. 25.
11. *History of the Sterilization of the Feeble-Minded, Faribault Superintendent Correspondence*, Sterilization file, ca. 1940.
12. *ibid.*
13. *ibid.*
14. Faribault State School and Hospital, record of sterilization cases.
15. Letter, E. Enberg, Superintendent to Carl Swanson, Director Department of Social Security, April 16, 1940 Faribault Superintendent subject files, sterilization.
16. *History of the Sterilization of the Feeble-Minded, Faribault Superintendent Correspondence*, Sterilization file, ca. 1940.

17. Letter, psychologist to Social Security Division, Public Welfare, Psychological Services, October 23, 1947.
18. History of the Sterilization of the Feeble-Minded, Faribault Superintendent Correspondence, Sterilization file, ca. 1940.
19. *Minnesota School for Feeble-Minded and Colony for Epileptics Farbault and Colony for Epileptics Cambridge,* June 30, 1928, p. 5.
20. Letter, Mildred Thomson to Dr. E Enberg July 22, 1958. Owatonna State School—Sterilization file.
21. Letter, Mildred Thomson to Dr. McBroom, October 31, 1929, Cambridge Correspondence.
22. Public Welfare, Psychological Services, Some State Laws, Policies of Board of Control, and Rules of Division of Research, January 11, 1935.
23. Letter Director Research Bureau to A. Leahy, Institute of Child Welfare February 26, 1931, Public Welfare—Psychological Services.
24. Sauk Centre Home School for Girls, case files.
25. Engberg, E. "The treatment of Mental Defectives in Minnesota." *Minnesota Medicine* vol 23, p. 335- 338, May 1940, Public Welfare Feeble-Minded Miscellaneous, MHS.
26. Faribault State School and Hospital admission records.
27. Ripley, Martha. "History of Fifty Years Service to Mothers and Babies in Minneapolis," *Bulletin for 1956.* Maternity hospital.
28. "No. cases seen by Bureau July 1, 1941-July 1, 1942," Public Welfare, Psychological Services.
29. Speech by C. Lowe from the Research Bureau to State Conference on Social Work September 1926, Public Welfare—psychological services.
30. Faribault State School and Hospital Biennial Reports, 1940, 1942, 1944.
31. Ripley, Martha. "History of Fifty Years Service to Mothers and Babies in Minneapolis," *Bulletin for 1956.* Maternity hospital.
32. Faribault, *Biennial Report,* June 1940.
33. Letter Mildred Thomson to E. Enberg August 31, 1943 Faribault Superintendent subject files—letters.
34. Letter, Mildren Thomson to Dr. Murdoch, October 25, 1930, Cambridge correspondence.
35. E. Engberg. "The Treatment of Mental Defectives in Minnesota," *Minnesota Medicine,* May 1940, p. 335.
36. Faribault Correspondence, to Dr. Enberg, January 15, 1942.
37. Letter, George Eitel, M.D. to E. Enberg. September 13, 1938, Faribault superintendent correspondence, sterilization file.
38. Faribault, Record of Sterilization cases 1916-1937.
39. Letter, Dr. Murdoch to Dr. McBroom March 28, 1931, Cambridge correspondence.
40. Faribault, Record of Sterilization cases 1916-1937.
41. Letter E. Enberg, Superintendent to E. Webster. Faribault Superintendent subject files, sterilization.
42. *Biennial Report of the Children's Bureau.* June 30, 1928, p. 18.

43. Letter, Mildred Thomson to Dr. McBroom February 5, 1931, Cambridge Correspondence.
44. Ladd-Taylor, Molly. "Eugenic Sterilization in Minnesota." *Minnesota History*, Summer 2005, v. 59:6.
45. *Biennial Report of the Children's Bureau,* June 30, 1930.
46. Faribault State Hospital and School, "Medical Staff Minutes 1936."
47. State of Minnesota Supreme Court, "Opinion and Syllabus, March 3, 1944."
48. *Biennial Report of the Children's Bureau,* June 30, 1936, p. 24.
49. *A Continuative Census and Registration of the Febble-Minded Public Welfare,* Bureau Feeble-Minded, ca. 1933.
50. *History of the Sterilization of the Feeble-Minded,* Faribault Superintendent Correspondence, Sterilization file, ca. 1940.
51. Letter, R Bowman to Carl Swenson, October 16, 1945, Faribault State Hospital and School Superintendent subject files, sterilization.
52. Letter to Dr. Enberg from Dr. Cameron. November 20, 1957, Faribault Superintendent Subject File, sterilization.
53. Faribault, Record of Sterilization cases 1916-1937.
54. *A Continuative Census and Registration of the Feeble-Minded Public Welfare,* Bureau Feeble-Minded, ca. 1935.
55. Letter, E. Enberg to Carl Swanson. April 16, 1940, Faribault superintendent correspondence, sterilization file..
56. Public Welfare, Psychological Services, ca. 1944.
57. Thomson, Mildred. Prologue. *A Minnesota story of Mental Retardation Showing Changing Attitudes and Philosophies Prior to Setpember1, 1959.* Gilbert Publishing, Minneapolis, 1963, p. 183.
58. Dight Institute, 1950, University of Minnesota Archives.
59. Gamble C. J. *American Journal of Psychiatry,* 107:932-934, June 1951.
60. *Sterilizations Reported in the US to January 1, 1954.* Human Betterment Association of America. University of Minnesota Archives.
61. Dight Institute, University of Minnesota Archives.
62. *Minnesota History,* Summer 2005.

CHAPTER ELEVEN
PASSIVE EUTHANASIA

THERE IS NO EVIDENCE, AND NOTHING TO SUGGEST, that an intention existed at any level of state government to deliberately kill state hospital patients. However, conditions of severe neglect resulted in many deaths through suicide and poor medical care. The death of a patient meant the end of their expense to society.

Calling this "passive euthanasia" and applying it to Minnesota state hospitals may seem harsh, but the term had been widely linked to institutional deaths as early as 1915. At this time, a Chicago physician withheld treatment for a handicapped newborn, justifying his actions on the death rates in Illinois state facilities for the feeble-minded. His actions were subsequently publicized in a Hollywood film.[1]

During the first half of the twentieth century, patients died in some Minnesota state hospitals an average of two per week.[2]

State hospitals were subject to the same infectious diseases as the rest of society, and the hospitals' responses were not always effective. Typhoid fever was an ongoing problem early in the 1900s at Faribault. An inmate went home on a vacation and a later investigation revealed that he returned with typhoid. He was assigned to the dairy, and infected the dairyman. The milk became contaminated and fifty-seven patients contracted the disease. As soon as it appeared, inoculations were given to 1,520 patients and staff. The mortality rate among those vaccinated was 9.1 percent, compared to twenty-three percent of the unvaccinated. The milk was sterilized for four weeks. Despite the seriousness of the outbreak, little was done to screen the health of inmates as they were admitted or returned from vacation. A year later, three inmates were admitted with symptoms of typhoid. Soon there were nine cases, three of whom died.[3]

Epidemics that swept the country showed up in the institutions as well. Influenza hit the Faribault hospital hard in 1918, affecting almost a third of the population, with a death rate of eleven percent.[4] This was over four times the mortality rate in the general U.S. population.[5] Whether this was due to vulnerability of inmates because of their physical disabilities, crowded conditions, or lack of treatment resources is unclear.

Other deaths occurred because every Minnesota state hospital was located adjacent to a body of water, railroad tracks, or both. Patients got out of locked buildings and killed themselves on the tracks and in the water. The second leading cause of death listed in the Cambridge State Hospital 1948 Biennial Report was drowning.[6] The Cambridge superintendent's request for $12,600 to build a fence along the river was approved.[7]

None of the other state hospitals had fenced off these hazards by the time they closed in the 1980s. It is interesting that Cambridge, which at the time housed only epileptic patients, provided some protection from suicides and the hospitals with psychiatric patients, some of whom were suicidal, did not.

Medical care was not always readily available or administered, and injuries could occur with frightening regularity. Patients put their fists through unprotected windows, causing severe cuts. They broke their hips in slippery showers and got boils from sharing the few towels that were available. Stair railings were missing and not replaced.[8] Medications for seizures and insulin for diabetes were available at some hospitals, but with no dieticians on staff, special diets were not provided.[9] Anything beyond simple surgery required a transfer to a medical hospital, which was done only after the family agreed to pay expenses. Cancers went untreated, with morphine the only intervention. Bed sores became gangrenous.[10] In fact, medical care was so limited that in one case, a diabetic patient with ulcers on both feet and a fractured hip was moved out of the infirmary into a 200-bed regular ward to make room for patients who were more in need of care.[11]

Tuberculosis in Ah-Gwah-Ching

Ah-Gwah-Ching was the only state institution serving exclusively as a tuberculosis sanatorium. Treatment for patients with TB centered, during the early 1900s, on repairing the lungs by encouraging the formation of tubercles

Footbridge over railroad tracks, St. Peter State Hospital ca 1908, courtesy of Nicollet County Historical Society. Note the lack of fencing along the train tracks.

encapsulating acute infections. This was done through providing fresh air, good food , rest and eventually exercise. Once encapsulated, the infection was considered healed. The patient's spitum would no longer contain TB bacteria, so they wouldn't infect others. They would continue to carry the disease but were considered cured and could be discharged.

Fresh air was thought to be helpful because of its tonic effect on the entire body. Sleeping areas were unheated to provide more fresh air. During the winter, the temperature in the sleeping porches reached thirty-seven degrees below zero. Windows were sometimes left open and during storms, beds were covered with snow. Nurses wore coats and mittens to care for patients.[12]

The open air buildings were nicknamed "Seldom Inn" or "Hard Times." Bathrooms were located in central areas, which were heated with barrel stoves. Patients brought crockery jugs of hot water they called "pigs" to bed to help keep warm,[13] and recounted using as many as seventeen blankets and waking up to find them covered with ice.[14]

Rest was important because it was felt that tubercles would form faster when the lungs moved as little as possible. Patients were positioned to lie on the infected side so their ribs moved less. Strict bed rest was the rule until

TB sanitarium, Faribault School for Feeble-Minded ca 1910, courtesy Minnesota Historical Society. The benefits of segregating infected patients was recognized, but these efforts were overwhelmed by later overcrowding.

their fever was below 100 degrees. They were then kept in bed for at least as long as it had taken to get their fever down. This could be six months or a year.

Exercise consisted of first allowing them to go to the toilet. They were then allowed to go to the dining room, at first for only one meal a day every other day. This was gradually increased until they were eating all meals in the dining room. They were then allowed a five-to-ten-minute walk, which was increased up to four hours of exercise a day. Their temperatures were monitored daily, and if it climbed to ninety-nine degrees for three days, the exercise was reduced. If it rose to over 100 degrees, they were put back on bed rest. After four to six months of exercising four hours a day, patients were discharged.[15]

Occupational therapy was considered very beneficial to keep patients quiet and contented. They were also provided with industrial rehabilitation to learn less strenuous occupations.[16]

The sanatorium at Ah-Gwah Ching kept up with improvements in medical care. The fresh air treatment was replaced in 1918 by heliotherapy, and the first thoracoplasty was carried out by a Mayo Clinic physician. Two years later, an X-ray machine was installed.[17] Major surgeries began in 1939.[18] Streptomycin was introduced in 1947, but thoacoplastic surgeries continued.[19]

By the mid 1920s, the facility had expanded to a capacity of 325. Bus service replaced rail transportation and the train depot was torn down in 1933.[20] The 1930s saw a number of improvements in the physical plant and operation. The first residence for nurses was completed in 1930.[21]

The medical director instituted a hospital technique regimen designed to protect employees from infection in 1932.[22] Prior to this, staff and patients mingled. Now, employees were required to wear gowns and masks. Ambulatory patients with positive sputum tests were a hazard in the dining room, so a separate dining room with cafeteria-style steam table was built in 1932.[23]

Objects were considered to be possible agents of disease transmission, and library books were washed and checked with ultraviolet light. Money in the patient store was ironed to kill germs.[24]

In the early 1930s, children were no longer admitted. It was felt that bringing them into an institution was causing more harm than good.[25]

Children's Cottage, sanitarium, undated, courtesy Minnesota Historical Society. Note the open windows—and this is northern Minnesota! Fresh air was considered therapeutic, so patients slept in unheated cottages under as many as seventeen blankets.

Congress granted $225,000 for constructing a building to house Native Americans in 1933, which brought the total capacity of the sanitarium to 480. Some Native American patients snuck out to attend pow-wows or to go ricing, so a locked unit was created in the basement.[26]

The institution included a farming operation. In the 1930s, they had the largest herd of registered Holstein cattle in northern Minnesota and sold some to local farmers for their own dairy herds. In addition to producing and pasteurizing the milk they needed, the sanatorium raised their own potatoes and vegetables.[27] In 1947, they received onions, potatoes, tomatoes and beef from Fergus Falls State Hospital and sent turkeys, hay, hogs and lard to six state facilities.[28] Patients not on bed rest often fished in Leech Lake, sometimes needing a horse and wagon to bring in their catch.[29]

The open wooden building called "Seldom Inn" was sold in 1947 for $500.00. The sanatorium was directed to create a locked unit to house TB patients who refused treatment and posed a threat to the public. The superintendent's 1951 report said it was a farce which accomplished nothing. Calling it a "tissue paper Bastille," he claimed that as many patients were at large as before the doors and windows were barred.[30]

A decline in patient population was seen for the first time in 1954. Two years later, thirty senile women with TB were transferred from Anoka State

Cottage A, sanitarium, ca. 1913, courtesy Minnesota Historical Society.

Sanitarium train station, ca 1915, courtesy Minnesota Historical Society. Trains carried patients to the sanitarium until adequate roads and bus systems were developed.

Hospital. By 1958, forty-three percent of the beds were filled with committed senile patients from state hospitals, one-third of whom had TB. The facility became a state nursing home in January 1, 1962, for senile mental patients. The TB patients who remained were transferred to Glen Lake. Medical staff were reduced to one physician, and staff housing was converted for patients, increasing the bed capacity to 423.[31]

TUBERCULOSIS IN OTHER STATE HOSPITALS

FROM VERY EARLY ON, TUBERCULOSIS WAS prevalent and deadly in state institutions. It was the leading cause of death at Faribault during the years 1902 -1908, with ninety cases. Epilepsy followed with fifty-five. Other causes of death were in the single digits.[32]

Many TB patients died while in their early teens, though children as young as four, five, and six years old died of TB.[33] In response, a tuberculosis hospital building was constructed at Faribault in 1906. Described at the time as the most satisfactory building on the grounds, it provided outdoor courtyards, forced ventilation, large windows, tile floors and a steam sterilizer.

This laudable effort was abandoned in 1924, when the building was needed to house feeble-minded patients on the Faribault waiting list. TB patients were transferred to the general hospital on the grounds.[34]

The ability to construct suitable buildings to care for patients with TB had been demonstrated at Faribault at the turn of the century. Sixteen years later, the state hospital directors urged the development of TB sanatoria in state institutions.[35] Another fifteen years would pass until a survey was carried out in state hospitals, revealing large numbers of patients with TB. During that thirty years, hundreds of patients with TB continued to be housed with the general state hospital populations.

Sanatoriums in Minnesota were treating acute TB in the early 1920s through bed rest, until the infections were encapsulated and patient's spitum cleared. They found that all TB patients who developed infections in their mouths, sinuses or tonsils required surgical intervention. TB sanatoriums reported, "Astonishing results, both symptomatic and physical, are often obtained from bed rest in the early stage of the treatment . . ."[36]

Despite the good results being obtained in Minnesota sanitariums, TB patients inside state hospitals weren't isolated or treated. The lack of isolation didn't occur only within hospitals, though; the presence of TB apparently wasn't part of the consideration process when patients were transferred between hospitals. State hospital patients were transferred and then returned in many cases because they had active TB.[37]

Dr. H. Burns was superintendent of the State Sanatorium in 1934, and studied the incidence of TB in state institutions. Demonstrating the widespread exposure to TB, eighty-three percent of Anoka patients reacted positively to a Mantoux Test. On subsequent X-rays of those who responded positively, sixty-four percent were found to have evidence of first infection or reinfection. Frequent X-rays and isolation of active cases were recommended.[38]

Willmar found two employees and 173 patients with pulmonary TB. Seventeen additional cases were identified in the following year and a half. An additional five cases were discovered during autopsies.[39]

Following this survey, units were developed in some state hospitals to segregate and treat TB patients. Other institutions transferred patients to these units. Faribault transferred out fifty-five TB patients between 1934 and 1943, and then set up its own TB unit. One hundred nine patients died from TB in Faribault during those ten years.

St. Peter responded three years later by segregating TB patients in two buildings. Staff working in these areas were given chest X-rays every three months.[40] The mere creation of these wards doesn't tell the whole story, however. Twelve years after the isolation unit had been created, St. Peter still had not addressed the isolation needs an active TB ward required. For example, the containers used to transport food to the wards and the laundry presented contamination hazards to staff and healthy patients. In addition, the women's ward was on the second floor with no elevator, making it difficult to transport bed patients.[41]

Hastings was unable to effectively respond to the 1934 TB survey, but a 1940 patient survey found that twenty-two had active TB and another fifty were quiescent. The superintendent wrote to the director of public institutions, saying,

> It is imperative that these patients be segregated so that they may be given special care and so that they will not infect other inmates or employees. We respectfully request permission to transfer these patients to one of the other state hospitals where isolation units are available. In the event that no beds are available in these other institutions it will be necessary for us to have additional help in order to give proper care for these patients who have a contagious disease as well as mental illness. (We do not have one trained nurse taking care of these t.b. patients.)[42]

Dr. Burns's survey prompted the screening of all new employees for TB, first with a Mantoux test and, in 1939, by chest X-ray. Mantoux tests and X-rays were given to all new patients, with gastric lavage studies done for any positive results. One employee applicant had been in a sanatorium but was thought to have an arrested case of TB. Her X-ray led to a diagnosis of stage one TB, and she was discharged from temporary employment.

The TB ward at Anoka was inadequate in 1945. Patients provided care for each other without any sanitary techniques. The wooden floor couldn't be kept clean. There was no sink, so dishes were washed in a dish pan. Showers were in the basement and the only tub in the attic, so patients were given baths by being hosed down while sitting on the toilet. An inspector commented, "Heaven help us if this is ever made public."[43]

In, 1948, the legislature appropriated $92,000 to remodel a building at Anoka for TB patients from other state hospitals. The head of public institutions felt this appropriation was too low, and that it would require $442,000 to renovate and equip the building for the 300 known TB cases in the system. Problems involved included updating food handling and laundry.[40] Supplies for the new facility were so short that the director of public institutions wrote to other state hospitals asking for caps, gowns and masks to use in their TB wards. He also wanted any isolation dresses or trousers they could spare. Because not enough non-tubercular patients had yet been sent out of Anoka, they needed beds as well.[45]

A twenty-six-bed unit was created in Anoka to house recalcitrant TB patients in December of 1958. People with TB living in the community who refused treatment or were too difficult to manage in county sanatoria were admitted under district court commitment. It turned out that all the beds weren't needed, so patients from penal institutions were included. In June 1960, it housed thirteen patients.[46]

The TB unit at Anoka was closed in 1967. Glen Lake State Sanatorium became the facility for patients of state institutions—including correctional institutions—who required special care, and for district court committed recalcitrant tuberculosis patients. TB patients classified as active and on drug therapy were kept in their home institutions. Glen Lake had difficulty detaining patients from corrections and those committed as recalcitrant.[47]

Tuberculosis spread in the state hospitals. The Commissioner of Mental Health in 1950 stated, "There is a shockingly high incidence of tuberculosis in the State Hospitals, among 14,000 patients there are over 450 cases of tuberculosis requiring special treatment. In part, at least, this situation reflects the sins of the past—overcrowding, lack of segregation, inadequate general medical services and lack of vigorous treatment."[48]

Dr. H.A. Burns, the state tuberculosis control officer for state institutions, stated he had nothing to work with and could not get rid of TB under existing conditions. Hospitals are unable to isolate patients or provide treatment. The "Minnesota Bedlam" series stated, "Dr. Burns, a tall, sad-eyed man, has just about given up hope that anything will be done to get rid of tuberculosis in the mental institutions. When he first took over the TB control unit in 1942, he recommended specific changes. Nothing was done. He has made those recommendations innumerable times since, but they have encouraged no action."[49]

The results of this inaction are demonstrated in the table on the following page, presented to the legislature in 1950. Efforts were made in institutions to identify and treat TB patients. They resulted in a decline, but death rates continued to be approximately forty times that of the general population. Minnesota was operating several TB sanitariums at the time, but this table includes only institutions for the mentally ill.

The 1946 Anoka budget request included an isolation cattle barn to be used to separate sick cows from the rest of the herd, but the move to remodel a cottage to use for TB patients didn't happen for several more years.[50]

While the public may have been unaware of what when on behind the walls of the state hospitals, state government was not. Monthly reports and detailed justifications for increased appropriations kept the central office well informed of how bad things were.

Failure to provide for the basic health and safety needs of patients may not have been the result of a policy of euthanasia, but an indifference to the survival of the insane was in keeping with eugenics.

TUBERCULOSIS DEATH RATES PER 100,000 IN MINNESOTA AND STATE INSTITUTIONS FOR THE MENTALLY ILL.[51]

Year	Minnesota	Mental Institutions
1936	35.6	1172.7
1937	33.5	1060.9
1938	29.7	940.6
1939	29.1	1292.9
1940	27.3	1004.2
1941	27.1	1142.3
1942	25.8	1080.6
1943	28.7	983.5
1944	26.9	914.7
1945	24	760.4
1946	21.2	661.2
1947	20.3	821
1948	17.1	527.8
1949	13.6	445.7
1950	10	431.7

NOTES

1. Black, Edwin. *War Against the Weak, Four Walls Eight Windows*. NY, 2003, p.252-258.
2. *Eleventh Biennial Report*, 1900.
3. Quarterly Conference of Executive Officers of State Institutions, 1915, pp. 13, 14.
4. *A Brief History of Minnesota's Mental Retardation Institutions*, ca. 1973, Faribault historical data files.
5. M Billings, 2005, http.virus.stanford.edu.
6. *Cambridge Biennial Report*, June 30, 1948.
7. *Cambridge Biennial Budget*, 1947-1948.
8. Anoka staff conference minutes, 1948.
9. Minneapolis *Tribune*, May 18, p. 10.

10. Anoka staff conference minutes, 1948.
11. Public Welfare Dept, Dr. Royal Gray, correspondence, 1950.
12. Oliver, Skip. *A Brief History of the Minnesota State Sanatorium*, June 1982, p. 6.
13. AhGwahChing Oral History transcripts—Clifford Bilben.
14. AhGwahChing Oral History transcripts—Carl Noren.
15. Dr.Mariette E. "Glen Lake Sanatorium and the Treatment Employed There," reprinted from *The Journal-Lancet*, March 1, 1922. Glen Lake Published Reports.
16. *ibid.*
17. Oliver, Skip. *A Brief History of the Minnesota State Sanatorium*, June 1982, p. 8.
18. *ibid.* p. 17.
19. *ibid.* p.19.
20. *ibid.* p.12.
21 *ibid.* p. 10.
22. *ibid.* p. 12.
23. AhGwahChing Annual Report 1932.
24. AhGwahChing Oral History transcripts—Clifford Bilben.
25. Oliver, Skip. *A Brief History of the Minnesota State Sanatorium*, June 1982, p.11
26. AhGwahChing Oral History transcripts—Clifford Bilben.
27. *ibid.*
28. AhGwahChing Annual Report 1947.
29. AhGwahChing Oral History transcripts—Carl Noren.
30. Ag-Gwah-Ching Annual Report 1951.
31. Oliver, Skip. *A Brief History of the Minnesota State Sanatorium*, June 1982, p. 23.
32. Faribault, Research 1902-1916.
33. Faribault State Hospital and School, "Record of Tuberculosis Patients Since Institution Began."
34. Enberg E. "The Problem of Controlling Tuberculosis in a Public Institution." Reprinted from The *American Journal of Mental Deficiency XLIX*, January 1945. Glen Lake Published Records.
35. *Biennial Report Hospitals and Asylums for the Insane Minnesota*, June 30, 1922 p. 5.
36. Mariette E. "Glen Lake Sanatorium and the Treatment Employed There," *The Journal-Lancet*, March 1, 1922.
37. Faribault State Hospital and School, "Record of Tuberculosis Patients Since Institution."
38. Gardner, W. "Pulmonary Tuberculosis Among Patients at Anoka (Minnesota) State Hospital, 1934-1941." *American Journal of Psychiatry*, 101, 3 November 1944, pp. 370-374.
39. *Biennial Report Of the Institutions for the Insane of the State Board of Control of Minnesota*, June 30, 1936, p. 17.
40. *Biennial Report Of the Hospitals for the Insane of Minnesota*, June 30, 1938 p. 42.
41 Letter A Krieser M.D. Head, Tuberculosis Control Unit to Dr. R. Rossen, Commissioner of Mental Health April 28, 1950. Public Welfare, Tuberculosis Control file.
42. Letter, Hastings Superintendent to Carl Swanson, August 20, 1940, Public Welfare Correspondence, Hastings.

43. Visitation Record, Anoka State Hospital, August 6, 1945, Social Security Department.

44. Letter, Carl Jackson to Governor Youngdahl, November 19, 1948. Governor Youngdahl Records, Public Institutions.

45. Letter, Carl Jackson to superintendent St. Peter May 28, 1951, Public Welfare Records, Anoka.

46. *MN Welfare Report,* Winter, 1960 p. 58.

47. *MN Welfare Report,* Winter, 1968 p. 57.

48. Office of the Commissioner of Mental Health, "The New Minnesota Mental Health Program," 1950.

49. Minneapolis *Tribune,* May 20, 1948, p. 8.

50. Control Board Published Records, *Itemized Statement of Recommendations for Appropriations Biennium,* 1947-1949.

51. Office of the Commissioner of Mental Health, *13th Biennial Report,* 1950 Legislative Reference Library.

CHAPTER TWELVE
LIFE ON THE WARDS

Eugenic principles resulted in the long-term commitment of many patients, causing overcrowding. In an effort to operate economical facilities, the conditions often associated with the "bad old days" in state hospitals developed. Each hospital became a self-sustaining small town, with as few staff as practicable.

PATIENT LIFE

The commitment process could begin with a complaint signed by almost anyone. The first that most patients knew of it was when the sheriff showed up to take them into custody. Some weren't even given time to dress before being hustled off to jail, where they awaited a court hearing. They may not have been told anything about what was going on, and had no legal representation. A judge and two physicians—who often weren't psychiatrists—would conduct the hearing. If committed, the sheriff would then transport the patient to the hospital.

Patients could only be released from commitment to someone who would officially take responsibility for them, usually a family member. This created an opportunity for people to get rid of their spouses. A confused, angry individual hauled out of their home and into court for no apparent reason would find it difficult to present themselves well. Given some damning testimony submitted from their husband or wife, they were at risk for being committed.

Hospital records include a number of wives committed because of the "delusion" that their husbands abused them. Said to be stubborn, sullen and mad at the world, they displayed no other signs of mental illness.[1]

The legal system thus participated in a form of prolonged spousal abuse. Once in the hospital, the spouse could keep them there by simply refusing to sign them out.

State hospitals typically put little stock in anything patients said. Nonetheless, the record includes anecdotal stories of patients who appeared perfectly normal. Some were never able to leave, forced to make what life they could for themselves.

When a patient entered, they were given a bowl haircut. All their possessions, including clothing, would be taken away. Patients were issued a dress made at the hospital and some socks. No underwear. Men would be issued a shirt, overalls and socks. On the once or twice weekly bath days, patients lined up, naked, in the hall to wait their turn for a shower. There'd be only two or three towels for the entire ward, resulting in epidemics of boils. There was no privacy in the bathroom, no toilet paper or even toilet seats.

The institutions were so large that supervision was challenging. An inspector noted at Anoka that the laundry man took little interest in his work. Commenting on the condition of the clothes, he said, "They do not show 'tattle-tale grey' but worse, they were a light brown."[2]

There was no way to deliver the food quickly to each ward, so it would be lukewarm, largely consisting of boiled vegetables, sometimes unrecognizable. Patients ate from a metal bowl with a smaller bowl for drinking. Some patients went hungry when nurses were alone with bedridden patients, because there was no way to get food trays up to the wards.[3]

At night, the beds were lined up end to end, with barely enough room to squeeze between. If the hos-

Christmas at St. Peter, ca. 1937, courtesy of Nicollet County Historical Society. Staff did what they could to help patients celebrate holidays.

Auditorium decorated for Christmas, St. Peter State Hospital 1913, Courtesy Nicollet County Historical Society. Each hospital used similar large spaces for movies and musical events—some put on by patients, and others by visiting groups.

pital was very crowded, patients might sleep in an attic, porch or basement that was unheated or inadequately ventilated. If a patient was lucky, their bed had two sheets and a blanket, though some had to make do with one sheet and part of a torn blanket. Patients couldn't escape the smell in the sleeping area—soiled mattresses were not replaced very often, and most wards included bedridden patients.

It may have been just as well that patients had nothing, for there was no place to put anything. Patients wearing glasses had to guard them. If they were lost or broken, their family would have to pay to replace them. As late as 1950, hospitals still hadn't taken responsibility for providing dentures or glasses to patients.[4]

These conditions resulted in horrific environments for patients. If they were lucky, they worked. The others stayed locked on the ward, forced to do nothing all day, every day. At least the patients who worked got shoes to wear and a change of scenery. Chances were, they could talk with the people they worked with, too. Patients assigned to the kitchen might grab some extra food, maybe even some of the good stuff they fed staff. Some farm managers supplied their guys with tobacco.

Patients in the ward could be surrounded with a variety of dangerous and deteriorated patients. Some would be in restraints, wailing and moaning. Many patients were senile or experiencing the end stages of alcoholism or syphilis. Few could carry on a conversation, and even fewer could form friendships. Patients were alone, with nothing to do. In some cases, there may not be enough places to sit, and patients weren't allowed anywhere near the beds, so they had to stand, or pace. The one or two attendants couldn't keep up with patient's toileting needs, so the smell would be horrible.

Worst of all for the patients would be the knowledge that each day would be like this for the rest of their lives. Patients who protested how they were being treated, demanded or even kept requesting to write a relative or get on a work crew, were considered troublesome. Cooperation and silence ensured patients were left alone. Bothering staff could put a patient on the slide to seclusion and a series of more restrictive restraints or sedatives.

Root cellar, St. Peter State Hospital, ca. 1910, courtesy of Nicollet County Historical Society. Patients on the grounds crew preferred to get off the wards, even in bad weather. They nicknamed it their hotel.

Demonstrating competence, smiling and being gracious would at most get patients a job, if one was available. Nothing would get them home.

Patients with a great deal of mental and emotional toughness who were able to work kept themselves together for many years. They independently performed skilled tasks, helping to operate machinery in the kitchen, laundry and farm. Beautiful, complex handwork was produced in occupational therapy, under what one superintendent termed slave labor conditions.[5]

Hospitals provided what entertainment they could. In the 1930s, Fergus Falls had a beauty parlor that served 500 women per month; a library with 4,000 volumes; diversional therapy where pictures, table runners and tablecloths, curtains and costumes for patient plays were made; silent movies once per week attended by five to six hundred patients; radios in seventeen wards; pianos; and billiard tables on two of the men's wards.

Patients gave choral performances at the local high school auditorium and for the Parents and Teachers' Association. On two occasions, they performed for the local radio station. Various organizations, including high schools, the American Legion and local orchestra, came to the hospital and performed for patients. Patients played baseball twice a week.[6]

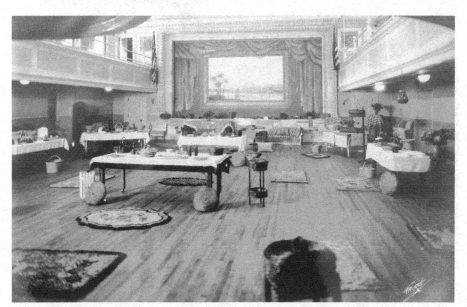

Faribault School and Hospital, ca. 1927, courtesy Minnesota Historical Society. Industrial products, made by patients, for sale.

Cambridge provided games and recreations in the day rooms during the winter and walks in the summer. Every ward had a radio and phonograph, and each building a piano. Moving pictures were shown every other Saturday. Two dances or parties were held each week during the school year. In the summer, these were replaced by picnics. Patients often played baseball and kittenball.[7]

Despite a life sentence, being labeled defective and forced to live and work in a very strange environment, some patients adjusted and made a life for themselves. Those locked on the wards usually lost theirs.

People with epilepsy were committed, as were homosexuals. Temporary mental conditions such as postpartum depression, situational anxiety, hysteria or the depression resulting from a tragedy all could result in a permanent commitment. The individual may have been perfectly mentally and emotionally capable shortly after being admitted.

Who could survive being immersed on the ward?

An inspector commented on a thirteen-year-old patient at Moose Lake: "She is now being housed with a group of adult and senile women in

Male patients, Willmar State Hospital, ca. 1940, courtesy Minnesota Historical Society. The alternative to working was forced idleness in a day room.

various stages of agitation and deterioration. No attention can be given this child so far as training and schooling which might be of greater value in her mental condition under more satisfactory control. She is quite lost playing with her dolls and toys in this sort of environment."[8]

STAFF LIFE

FROM THE BEGINNING, STATE HOSPITAL STAFF were underpaid. Fergus Falls was able to report, in 1892, that due to increased wages they were now hiring people educated in training schools. The report stated, "We no longer employ the underpaid riff-raff and rolling stones of society. . . ."[9] That's quite a harsh criticism from the hospital superintendent of former staff who were frequently producing positive outcomes for patients.

In the 1900 biennial report, the Fergus Falls superintendent noted that,

> It therefore seems almost inevitable that the nurses who have the care of the chronic patients, whose work is simply a daily routine, much of it of an exceedingly disagreeable nature, keeping their charges cleanly, seeing that they are kindly treated, their necessities looked after, and interesting them in work and amusement, after a while show a lack of interest in the work, and fail to acquire a true hospital spirit.[10]

Attendants were required to live on the wards at St. Peter until 1907. They got only every other Sunday off and were paid less than half of prison guards. Staff were so difficult to recruit that a number of hospital patients were discharged and then immediately hired as staff, sometimes onto the same ward they'd been living on.[11]

In the earliest years at Rochester, the staff was composed only of one or two doctors in charge of the rest of the employees, who were all untrained assistants. No nurses were employed.[12] Later, conditions improved so staff worked only a forty-eight-hour week. On average, there were one-point-eight staff per ward on Anoka's women's wards, one-point-three on men's, with sixty-one patients per employee per shift. When the governor visited in 1948, he was not happy about finding a cottage that had forty-three patients on a ward in restraints with only one attendant.[13]

As mentioned above, part of what made the system work with so few staff was assigning patients to care for other patients.[14] Vacancies were hard to fill. In Anoka, when a night supervisor was taken suddenly ill, there was no one to take her place. Over a hundred patients were left unattended.[15]

A student nurse reported in a letter to her father in 1948:

> All you hear night and day is people screaming. And the food is terrible. Where we eat the smell of urine is so bad that if that doesn't get you, the food you may choke down will. We have been here nearly three weeks and we haven't had one fresh fruit or vegetable so if you want to really do me a favor, have the house loaded with lettuce and tomatoes, cucumbers, onions, etc. and cherries or any fresh fruit. I never want to see another pea or meat or potatoes as long as I live. As far as I'm concerned I'd never consent to *any* of my relatives ever being inmates of this dump. Just wait till I tell you some of the rot around here.[16]

Many employees lived on campus and were served an adequate and diversified diet. St. Peter maintained a number of separate kitchens, including one serving doctors and senior staff, another that served twenty-five staff, and a third just for student nurses.[17]

Sanitary conditions were not adequate, either. Staff at St. Peter would remove clean clothes from storage bins and find dead rats.[18] Roaches were found in the kitchen and wards at St. Peter during an inspection in 1910, blamed in part on rotted and warped wooden floors.[19] Staff remember that cockroaches came out at night, making walls look like they were moving when the lights were turned on. They had to wait after picking up a phone for the roaches to run out of the ear piece. When they arrived home, they slammed their lunch buckets down on their kitchen counter to make sure bugs hadn't caught a ride.[20]

Staff did the best they could in the face of low wages and limited numbers. A doctor inspected Hastings in 1942, and found that the surgical cottage was filthy. The ward nurse responded:

"Dear Dr. Rossen,

In regard to the letter of Dr. Orr's, I take this as a matter of personal insult. In as much as I don't think that Dr. Orr understands the difficulties that we are up against. The turn-over in help has been quite a problem. And when we do get new help they have to be trained as they are green as grass. This is a handicap as we only have enough men to run the cottage. Then when there is luetic treatments of C-4 or C-9 we have to send a man to them. This shorts us on this cottage. When we have surgery we have to assist and then clean up the surgery afterwards. Also we help put on casts, help set bones, help do spinal punctures and anoxia treatments in the surgery, not counting our work with sterilizing, cleaning syringes and equipment, fixing sponges, gloves and towels.

As far as the surgical ward is concerned, we have no choice as to whom we have to put in there. Involuntaries have to be kept there as well as clean patients. Also we can't open the windows in the surgical ward as Dr. Radabaugh ordered them blocked down tight. This was done and is still in force as far as we are concerned.

It has been around 6 weeks since we received any scouring powder. This in itself makes our soap go twice as fast and there was no increase in our soap allowance.

I am not trying to talk myself out of a situation but trying to explain the situation so that is can be understood and be given at least a little credit for what is done.

Another thing is this; that at the wages that employees get for working here on cottage 8 where they have more to do than on any other cottage and you start to push them to get it done they say they will quit as they aren't getting enough anyway and there are plenty of good jobs to be had outside. So, Dr.

Staff apartments, St. Peter State Hospital ca 1949, Courtesy of Nicollet County Historical Society. Living conditions for staff gradually improved. At first, they had to sleep on the wards.

Rossen, I hope that with this information you can explain to Dr. Orr.

Yours very sincerely,

(_____)[21]

As we can see, the list of tasks that had to be learned on the job is startling—helping set bones, do spinal punctures and sterilizing equipment. The anoxia treatments were potentially life-threatening for patients. New staff were given little orientation before being thrust into danger. A new nurse was left alone on her first afternoon on a violent women's ward. She'd heard that one of the patients on the ward had killed two nurses, but wasn't told who it was.[22]

Records of staff at Anoka being injured were sent monthly to Carl Swanson. They were hit, kicked, bitten and scratched by patients on a regular basis. A number of financial claims and hearings resulted. The note of an injury to an eighteen-year-old woman said, "Employee was putting a violent patient in camisole and the patient scratched employee's arm in the struggle."[23] What a picture—a young woman just out of high school with only on-the-job training, battling to put a straightjacket on a dangerous patient. It was a wonder they could recruit anyone to work in a state hospital.

PATIENT ABUSE

IN ADDITION TO THE INDIFFERENCE TO PATIENT suffering engendered by the lack of resources and options, patients were punished. Before rejecting these as examples of egregious cruelty, they should be placed in the existing milieu.

The Rochester hospital superintendent was ill during 1909, and was able only to make occasional rounds of the women's wards. Complaints were made to the Board of Visitors about staff drunkenness and cruelty to patients. An independent investigation substantiated the allegations and reported to the governor. The nursing staff involved left or were fired.[24] Both the use of an independent investigation process and the involvement of the governor's office show how serious these charges were considered.

At Faribault, the official response to discipline was measured and careful: "Cases seeming to require punishment are acted upon by the Superintendent or an officer, and coporal punishment is not delegated to any one. If in an extreme case it is required, the superintendent alone assumes the responsibility of such action."[25]

The actual practice a few years later was somewhat different. The discipline and restraint record states that two defiant male residents were spanked, a girl was locked in her room all day, several children were made to stay under the matron's bed for half a day, and others had to stand on a rug or behind the door for half an hour. A girl resisted taking a bath and when placed in the tub, she began screaming. The record documents the discipline given: "I got a cup and threw water in her face until she was glad to stop." A girl from the epileptic cottage fought with staff, and the record states, "I then pulled her back and slapped her face 4 or 5 times. Might have been more times and locked her in the quiet room."[26]

The employees' rules and regulations at Cambridge State Hospital said, "Force will seldom be necessary, but when it is, let it be exercised with tact and kindness, and accompanied with cheerful explanatory words and a sympathizing manner."[27] It's difficult to imagine that staff could use force according to this high standard.

State hospitals were dangerous places. Occasionally a strong, psychotic patient would seriously injure anyone nearby. Wards could become agitated and one or two staff could be confronted by fifty unpredictable people. It's not surprising that staff sought to "teach someone a lesson" when things got out of hand.

In answer to a reporter's question about abuse of patients, a hospital superintendent described a "restraint" that left no marks—a towel twisted tightly around a patient's throat. He said, "When I see a patient with extremely blood-shot eyes, I know what has happened." Another superintendent mentioned an attendant who walked the wards swinging and using a leather strap.[28] In neither instance was there an assurance from the superintendent that these practices had been discontinued. Instead, they were cited as examples of why staffing numbers and pay needed to be increased. In documented cases of abuse, aides were suspended for twenty days.[29]

In response to a patient's picking at her eyes and nose, during a staff meeting Anoka staff suggested putting a sock over her head. The doctor rejected this, pointing out that putting a sock or pillow case over someone's head was now against the rules. He stated that, ". . . one has been known to suffocate," and, "it is an old trick and it is not allowed."[30] The doctor's confirmation that patients had died in this manner is stunning. We might assume their hands were in some form of restraint, which prevented them from removing the sock or pillow case.

Aggression to objects or people wasn't necessary to trigger punishment. Patients who became verbally abusive were secluded.[31] When being locked in a seclusion room didn't work, patients were subjected to a harsher regimen. During their tours, the inspectors for the Unitarian Report cited the following example:

> Nude girl was found behind locked doors in seclusion room
> with her wrists and ankles tied to side of metal cot; the cot
> had no mattress; a thin blanket was between her body and

springs and folded over her; window wide open with outside temperature sub-zero. Nurse stated she was without
clothing and mattress because she was destructive. Observation: the girl was so completely bound it would have been
physically impossible for her to tear either clothing or mattress; she was visibly suffering from exposure.[32]

Restraints were sometimes kept on day and night for months at a time.
Patients were only released from them for an hour a week to take a bath.
They couldn't use their hands while restrained and had to be fed. Given the
shortage of staff, more capable patients were assigned to feed those in restraints. During the day, patients were tied to a bench, and at night, tied to
their bed.[33]

The use of restraints created some hazards. Numerous staff were injured while struggling to place patients in restraints. Leaving large numbers
of patients tied up with little supervision meant that restraints slipped. A
Willmar monthly casualty report included the following statement: "To our
sorrow one of our women patients died as a result of accidental strangula-
tion. She became twisted in a camisole jacket at night in one of our wards
for decrepits. The one nurse on duty was preoccupied with the needs of a
number of disturbed and untidy patients and was unable to make complete
rounds as frequently as called for."[34]

The Faribault medical staff minutes noted that a patient had been restrained in bed with a sheet folded one foot wide. He was found dead the
next morning with his feet out of bed and the sheet around his neck.[35]

It can be difficult for us to sort out treatments from punishment. Patients who refused to eat were sometimes given insulin to increase their ap-
petite. Disregarding how this would be medically viewed today, it appears
to have been a humane attempt to get them to eat. ECT was also used on
patients who didn't eat. This could have been viewed purely as a treatment
attempt, but given the fear many patients felt towards the treatment and the
common negative side effects, it could also have served as a powerful threat.

Tubes were put down patient's noses for feeding purposes if they
wouldn't eat. While still occasionally used today and seemingly benign, in

the Anoka State Hospital NG tubes were inserted and removed for each meal. In addition to increasing the risk, this greatly increased the discomfort and served to encourage patients to eat.[36] Patients at St. Peter ". . . gagged and squirmed all over the bed while the doctor tried to inch the tube down."[37]

Intimidation was used, as well. A Rochester staff member who was nearing retirement related to me (with some relish) a story of how male patients were processed on admission. A group of male staff gathered at shift change. The new patient was provoked by being jabbed in the crotch with a comb, ostensibly to check for lice. Then staff beat him with socks containing bars of soap. It was made very clear that violence to staff wouldn't be tolerated.

NOTES

1. Rubenstein, Bruce. "They Called Them Madhouses," *Minnesota Monthly*, February 1991, p. 44.
2. Visitation Record, Anoka State Hospita,l August 6, 1946, Social Security Department.
3. Anoka staff conference minutes, 1948.
4. Memo F. Nichols to Carl Jackson, April 10, 1950.
5. *The New MN Mental Health Program*, Office of the Commissioner of Mental Health, 1950
6. *Biennial Report Hospitals and Asylums for the Insane Minnesota*, June 30, 1932, p. 22, 23.
7. *Minnesota School for Feeble-Minded and Colony for Epileptics Farbault and Colony for Epileptics Cambridge* June 30, 1932, p. 13.
8. Visitation Record, Moose Lake State Hospital, December 28, 1946, Social Security Department.
9. *Seventh Biennial Report of the Board of Trustees and Officers of the Minnesota Hospitals for Insane*, July 31, 1892 p. 161.
10. *Eleventh Biennial Report Minnesota Hospitals for Insane*, June 1900.
11. Erickson, William. "Establishing Minnesota's First Hospital for the Insane," *Minnesota History*, Summer 1992, p. 54.
12. Wells, Lloyd. "Rural Psychiatry on the Nineteenth-Century Frontier: the Career of Jacob Bowers." *Perspectives in Biology and Medicine*, 1981, vol 24 pp. 270-83.
13. Anoka staff conference minutes, 1948.
14. St. Peter, L.B., oral history.
15. Visitation Record, Anoka State Hospital, August 6, 1945, Social Security Department.
16. Letter, student nurse to her father. Governor Youngdahl Records, Public Institutions, July 19, 1948.

17. Anoka staff conference minutes, 1948.
18. St. Peter, L.B., oral history.
19. *Second Biennial Report of the Minnesota State Board of Visitors for Public Institutions.* 1910, pp. 17, 18.
20. Hahn, Ruth. *Oh, You work at the Bughouse!* Taylor Publishing Co, Dallas, 1984, p. 92.
21. Letters, June 1942, Public Welfare Correspondence, Hastings.
22. Hahn, Ruth. Oh, *You work at the Bughouse!* Taylor Publishing Co, Dallas, 1984, p. 100.
23. Public Welfare Correspondence.
24. *Second Biennial Report of the Minnesota State Board of Visitors for Public Institutions.* 1910, pp. 11-15.
25. *Circular of Information Concerning the Minnesota School for Feeble-Minded & Colony for Epileptics,* 1905. Faribault, general administration 1901-1916.
26. Faribault Discipline and Restraint Record.
27. Cambridge Employee Rules and Regulations, circa 1929.
28. Minneapolis *Tribune,* May 15, 1948, p. 8.
29. Anoka staff conference minutes, 1948.
30. Anoka staff conference minutes, 1948.
31. Hahn, Ruth. *Oh, You work at the Bughouse!* Taylor Publishing Co, Dallas, 1984, p. 124.
32. Unitarian Report, page 10.
33. St. Peter, L.B., oral history.
34. Willmar State Hospital Monthly Reports, May 1954.
35. Faribault State School, medical staff minutes.
36. Anoka staff conference minutes, 1948.
37. Hahn, Ruth. *Oh, You work at the Bughouse!* Taylor Publishing Co, Dallas, 1984, p. 75.

CHAPTER THIRTEEN

INFRASTRUCTURE

STATE HOSPITALS IN MINNESOTA WERE essentially small villages. Patients—under the supervision of a few staff—grew and processed the food they ate. Most of the clothing, sometimes including shoes, was made on the grounds. Blankets were purchased, but mattresses and sheets where often produced in sewing shops. Some facilities even produced their own electricity using coal-driven DC generators.

INDUSTRY

PATIENTS WORKED AS MANY AS FOURTEEN hours a day, up to seven days a week, for no pay. The attitude of hospital staff toward patients' working can be seen in the following quote from 1892: "Many patients earnestly request such employment, but we have not enough land to give occupation to all who desire and would be benefited by it."[1]

Patients' efforts resulted in lowered costs for operating the state hospitals. The weekly per capita cost was $4.74 in Fergus Falls during the year ending July 31, 1894. This was expected to decrease as the hospital was completed and the hospital filled.[2] A $36,000 profit from the farm decreased the per capita cost at Faribault in 1917 to $145.00.[3] A staff member at the time wrote, "The services cheerfully rendered by the boys and girls on the farm, in the garden, in the shops, in keeping the buildings and ground in order, in the various housekeeping operations, and in fact, in all the departments of the institution have materially aided in keeping down the cost of operation."[4] Expenses per year were thus quite low.

Per capita costs were quite low across the board. In Faribault in 1928, the net per capita cost, listed as current expenses, was $201.17.[5] Per capita costs in the same year at Cambridge was $390.19.[6] The per capita costs at Cambridge drastically decreased by 1932, down to $206.02.[7] The net per capita costs hovered around there for the next decade, going as low as $174.77 in 1936,[8] and jumping back slightly to $191.43 in 1938. [9]

Not only did net per capita costs drop due to patients' work, but it was noted in Anoka that farm workers were underweight due to the amount of work they were performing.[10]

Among the equipment inventoried in the Rochester farm operation was a tobacco cutter. Likewise, in Fergus Falls, forty pounds of chewing tobacco was charged by the farm operation in April, 1950.[11] Other than getting off the ward, tobacco served as the only payment made for patients' labor.

In some cases, refusing to work resulted in losses such as movies or grounds privileges. At Anoka, patients could earn their way up to a liberty ward, or could be transferred to less desirable wards.[12] If they became belligerent or disrespectful they were subject to seclusion or restraint.[13] Those who were able, often chose to work.

Though it appeared to be in patients' best interests to work, they were sometimes injured at work from cuts and burns. After several incidents of men falling off open trucks, staff at Anoka commented that it was too bad the farm trucks didn't have sides.[14] There was no notation that this was going to be acted on.

Fire engine house, St. Peter State Hospital, ca. 1910, courtesy of Nicollet County Historical Society. Built before the city of St. Peter had a fire department, perhaps in response to the deadly fire that took place in 1880.

Patient labor was so necessary that they weren't always assigned to appropriate tasks. At Anoka, it was noted that a patient was becoming a nuisance because she was pulling her hair out near the food kettles.[15]

Patients weren't always well supervised while working, either. The 1948 Anoka budget request includes the following: "One Sauerkraut Cutter: $210.00. Our sauerkraut is now cut by hand by patients. Besides taking an excessive amount of time, this method is unsanitary as the men stand directly over the barrel and drop perspiration, tobacco, buttons and frequently pieces of clothing into the product." This rationale apparently wasn't persuasive enough, for the same item appears in the budget request two years later.[16] Menus aren't available to tell whether staff or only patients were served sauerkraut.

Activities at the Rochester hospital included: A shoe shop that repaired harnesses, made men's shoes, repaired shoes and made leather restraints; a sewing room and tailor shop that produced dresses, night gowns, table cloths, sheets, aprons, bibs, diapers and booties; a mattress and print shop; laundry; and a central kitchen and bakery. In season, crops were canned. In 1948, this included 9,302 gallons of corn and 911 gallons of pickles. In 1958, 1,634 cans of tomato juice, 5,587 cans of carrots and 2,800 cans of sauerkraut were processed. An occupational therapy shop produced items to be sold.[17]

The amount of work completed by patients was staggering. At St. Peter, they cut cordwood by hand, stacking it shoulder high in a line half a mile long.[18] In 1948, the Fergus Falls budget request included this rationale when asking for a steam shovel, saying,

> At the present time all coal is handled by hospital patients, unloading by hand and then wheeled to the elevator where it is conveyed to the coal hoppers. This crude way of handling the thousands of tons of coal is rather difficult as the scarcity of patient labor is becoming more and more acute. The dependable patients that are engaged in this work are the old standbys, who have been shoveling coal for many years. These men are arriving at the ages where the work is too strenuous for them, laboring in the bitter cold, heat and dust.[19]

Carpenter shop, St. Peter State Hospital, ca. 1960, courtesy of Nicollet County Historical Society. Repairs and furnishings were done on campus.

A coal conveyer was eventually built at Faribault to handle the 12,000 tons of coal that had been annually handled by resident labor.[20]

There was no patient retirement plan. The letter that opened this book referenced a seventy-year-old who was still working. A newspaper account noted an elderly woman carrying food up several flights of stairs.[21] The alternative to working remained the same: If you became unable to work, you returned to spend the rest of your days on the ward.

Unique to the Rochester campus was a limestone quarry, which generated approximately $38,000 per month in 1948 through 1950. The entire hospital payroll at the time was $36,000 per month.[22]

Occupational therapy operated as a production for sales unit. Patients who became proficient in a particular skill were kept in that assignment. Cambridge State Hospital, in 1938, made a profit of $922.95 at the State

Fair from sales of goods made in occupational therapy.[23] That might not sound like much, but when recalculated to match the increase in the fair's admission fee from twenty-five cents to eleven dollars, the amount comes to $40,609.80 in today's dollars.

Farm Operations

State hospitals were expected to grow their own food. These were labor intensive activities. In 1948 at Cambridge, 200 acres were under cultivation using only horse-drawn equipment. The superintendent requested funding to purchase more land because not enough animal feed and vegetables were being produced.[24]

In 1958, Rochester had forty-four male patients employed with farm duties—sixteen in the dairy, twenty on the farm and eight in the greenhouse. That fall they produced 18,681 pounds of pork, 2,009 pounds of chicken, 1,650 dozen eggs, 71,952 pounds of milk, 4,000 bushels of potatoes, 154 bushels of beets, 464 bushels of onions, 228 bushels of tomatoes, 336 bushels of carrots, 629 bushels rutabagas, 40,932 pounds of squash, and 68,116 pounds of cabbage.[25]

Greenhouse at St. Peter, ca. 1925, courtesy of Nicollet County Historical Society. State hospitals shared farm produce with other state institutions.

Ironing room, St. Peter State Hospital, ca. 1938, courtesy of Nicollet County Historical Society. Most clothing was made in house.

In 1949, livestock produced included eighty-one milk cows, fifty-four beef cattle, ten work horses, 183 pigs, 4,092 chickens and 1,504 turkeys. Animals were processed in a butcher shop on the grounds. The reported value of animals raised in 1948 was $36,852.00.

A groundskeeper at St. Peter was responsible for supervising work crews of as many as thirty-nine patients. Coordinating their work when patients were simultaneously driving eighteen pairs of horse-drawn plows or pushing thirty-nine individual lawn mowers was challenging. It could be dangerous, as well—the groundskeeper almost lost an ear when a patient hit him with a shovel. Staff depended on having at least one patient with them they could trust to watch their back.

Despite this, the work crews were a community. The men lined up each morning, eager to get off the wards. When the weather was bad, they hung out in the root cellar, a place they called their hotel. Years later, staff described members of the work crew as friends.

Employees cutting ice on the Minnesota River, St. Peter State Hospital, ca. 1940, courtesy of Nicollet County Historical Society. Used for the morgue and refrigerators, modern sensibilities cringe at using river water near food.

World War II led to manpower shortages both inside and outside the hospitals when male staff left for military service. Farms, local governments and factories needed help. St. Peter patients made surgical dressings for the Red Cross, producing over a thousand a month. Other patients worked outside the hospital, putting in over 6,000 hours on local farms, cleaning downtown and plucking chickens. They were paid standard rates, with wages placed in their patient accounts.[26]

Patients were also hired out to local governments and canning companies. They enjoyed earning thirty-five cents per hour. The staff liked it as well, for they pocketed $1.25 an hour in addition to their regular pay. Patients traveled to work sites by bus, sometimes stopping to buy beer on the way back.[27]

Utilities

From the beginning, getting enough money for utilities in the state hospitals was a struggle. At first, St. Peter lacked a clean water supply. The 1894 report urged that the plumbing and ventilation in the hospital be improved because, ". . . many cases of typhoid fever and dysentery have been

Mail wagon at St. Peter State Hospital, ca. 1908, courtesy of Nicollet County Historical Society. Many buildings were widely scattered across the grounds.

thought to be directly traceable to the defects in the sanitary condition of that hospital."[28]

Sewage was also a problem in Rochester during the early days. A small stream—Silver Creek—flowed through the north portion of the grounds. Originally, the hospital's sewage, including rags, scraps of food and other "putrescible animal and vegetable matter," were dumped into the creek. After ten years of this, the Rochester city council and local board of health met with hospital leaders to complain. The hospital defended itself by stating that their concerns didn't carry much weight because the banks of the stream weren't populated, but they agreed to refer the matter to the State Board of Health.

An inspection by the secretary of the State Board of Health determined that the present method created a nuisance, source of filth and possible cause of sickness. He stated that the practice must be stopped at once and ordered that all refuse be removed from the creek. His first advice was to run sewage into shallow ditches between growing crops, stating that this method was inexpensive and very efficient. If the ditches became offensive, they could be easily covered with a furrow. A better solution would be to install drain tiles under crops. He suggested installing them on the slope toward the ice pond, saying this would be far enough away from the water supply to present no danger.[29] (We have to hope that the ice pond was located above the slope, not below it.)

The hospital superintendent rejected these suggestions, instead requesting money for installing several cement settling tanks. The sewage water would then flow as an almost clear stream into the Zumbro River. He supported this request with the statement that this method was in vogue in several other similar institutions.[30]

At the Owatonna State School, disposing of sewage was also a problem: "At the present time sewage from the farm cottage, power plant and horse and cow barns runs into a separate sanitary sewer into an open gravel pit near Highway #7. This is very offensive especially in summer and will become worse in the future if the pit becomes clogged."[31]

State Fair exhibit, Fergus Falls, ca. 1915, courtesy Minnesota Historical Society. A significant amount of money was made selling hand work at the fair. Patients weren't paid, but materials could be purchased.

The water supply for Ah-Gwan-Ching came from Leech Lake, where it was collected from a sheltered bay and then chlorinated. Meanwhile, "... large volumes of sewage" were discharged into the main body of the lake.[32]

The Minnesota Department of Health noted, in 1941, that untreated waste was being discharged directly into the Rum River from the power plant toilet, the laundry and sinks of Anoka cottages one through four. This was especially a problem because dealers in Anoka were obtaining ice from the river adjacent to the waste outlets. In addition to recommending improvements to the sewer system, the Health Department said that ice used for domestic purposes should not be taken from the Rum River at Anoka.[33]

While discussions continued between the city of Anoka and the state about building additional sewage treatment facilities, sewers backed up into cottage basements at Anoka daily and dumped untreated waste into the river. In addition to inadequate facilities, limited maintenance created problems. An inspection by the industrial commission ordered better ventilation in a number of toilets at Anoka, and, "in the Cottages: Arrange so that all toilet bowls will flush with reasonable effort."[34]

The following justification was provided in the 1948 appropriation request for Hastings:

> After every heavy rain the sanitary sewers are overloaded and there is an overflow of from 2 to 4 inches of water into the basements. The main drainage pipe runs through our store room, and it is necessary for us to keep our supplies of perishable items on a platform approximately 6 inches high, and after these heavy rains, the store room is flooded by back wash from the combined sanitary and storm sewers, which is a detriment to our perishable items, such as soap, sugar, breakfast, etc. It is imperative for reasons just given, that we have separate storm and sanitary sewers on the east and west wings of the main building."[35]

State Fair display, Rochester, ca. 1910, courtesy Minnesota Historical Society.

Sewage was a problem as well at Fergus Falls. Two biennial requests reported that the bakery was located in a basement, at the same height as tunnels that flooded with sewage.[36]

Hospitals had other physical problems to deal with, too. Fires occurred at Anoka from obsolete electrical wiring. The main wires running between the power plant and the cottages ran through tunnels, were not encased in conduits, and in many places the insulation had worn off. Patients pushing metal food carts through the tunnels were at risk of being electrocuted. Front stairs and porches on several of the cottages had disintegrated and were hazardous. This necessitated using side or rear entrances ,which did not have sidewalks.[37]

Stoves in the kitchens were originally fired with coal. These were replaced with natural gas at St. Peter in the 1930s. The superintendent reported, "The most marked effect of the gas and the cleaning out of the flues has been the reduction of coal gas in the bakeshop itself. At times it used to be extremely uncomfortable to work there even though we had an exhaust fan. This has practically disappeared."[38] The smoke stack at Cambridge deteriorated so badly that the top fifty feet collapsed onto the boiler house, knocking a hole in the concrete ceiling.[39]

In cases of deaths, families were notified by collect calls.[38] Patients' bodies were then sent where their families wished for burial. As a final indignity, the Anoka State Hospital morgue used ice to cool bodies until they were claimed. However, the ice didn't keep them cold enough, and sometimes bodies were "ripe" by the time they left.[40]

NOTES

1. *Seventh Biennial Report of the Board of Trustees and Officers, of the Minnesota Hospitals for Insane*, July 31, 1892, p. 8.
2. *Eighth Biennial Report of the Board of Trustees and Officers of the Minnesota Hospitals for Insane*, July 31, 1894, p. 167.
3. *Brief History of Minnesota's Mental Retardation Institutions*, ca. 1973, Faribault historical data files.
4. *Minnesota School for Feeble-Minded and Colony for Epileptics Farbault and Colony for Epileptics Cambridge*, June 30, 1928, p. 8.
5. *Minnesota School for Feeble-Minded and Colony for Epileptics Farbault and Colony for Epileptics Cambridge*, June 30, 1928, p. 3.
6. *Ibid.*, p. 9.
7. *Minnesota School for Feeble-Minded and Colony for Epileptics Farbault and Colony for Epileptics Cambridge*, June 30, 1932, p. 11.
8. *Minnesota School for Feeble-Minded and Colony for Epileptics Farbault and Colony for Epileptics Cambridge*, June 30, 1936, p. 1.
9. *Minnesota School for Feeble-Minded and Colony for Epileptics Farbault and Colony for Epileptics Cambridge*, June 30, 1938, p. 2.
10. Anoka staff conference minutes, 1948.
11. Fergus Falls farm records.
12. Anoka Staff conference, 1948.
13. Cambridge discipline record.
14. Anoka staff conference minutes, 1948.
15. Anoka staff conference minutes, 1947.
16. Control Board, "Recommendations, Anoka," 1948.
17. Rochester State Hospital Monthly Reports.
18. St. Peter, R.L. oral history.
19. Control Board, "Recommendations, Fergus Falls," 1949.

20. *A Brief History of Minnesota's Mental Retardation Institutions,* ca. 1973, Faribault historical data files.
21. Minneapolis *Tribune,* May 14, 1948, p. 10.
22. Rochester Industrial Reports, 1948-1950.
23. Cambridge State Hospital correspondence.
24. Cambridge Biennial Budget 1947-1948.
25. Rochester Industrial Reports, 1958.
26. Monthly report, St. Peter SH, January 1944, September 1945, St. Peter SH Collection, Archives, Minnesota State University, Mankato.
27. St. Peter, R.L. oral history.
28. *Eighth Biennial Report of the Board of Trustees and Officers of the Minnesota Hospitals for Insane,* July 31, 1894, p. 4.
29. Fifth Biennial Report of the Board of Trustees and Officers of the Minnesota Hospital for the Insane, 1888, pp. 10-12.
30. *Ibid.*
31. Letter James Fitzsimmons to State Board of Control, March 1939, Owatonna State School.
32. Letter from Ah-Gwan-Ching to Minnesota Department of Health, April 14, 1938.
33. Minnesota Department of Health Division of Sanitation, December 10, 1941, Public Welfare Correspondence, inspection reports.
34. "Inspection report," Industrial Commission of Minnesota, March 5, 1943, Public Welfare Correspondence, Inspection Reports.
35. Control Board, "Recommendations, Hastings," 1948 .
36. Control Board, "Recommendations, Fergus Falls," 1943, 1945.
37. Itemized Statement of Recommendations for Appropriations, Control Board Published Records, ca. 1946, 1948.
38. Monthly report, St. Peter SH, October 1935, St. Peter SH Collection, Archives, Minnesota State University, Mankato.
39. Letter, Dr. McBroom to State Board of Control, May 23, 1930, Cambridge correspondence.
40. Anoka staff conference minutes, 1948.
41. Control Board, recommendations, Anoka, 1946.

CHAPTER FOURTEEN
MEDICAL CARE

NOWHERE WAS THE DISCREPANCY GREATER between what could have been, and what was, than the medical care at state hospitals. Funding, and therefore staffing, fluctuated, decreasing on a per capita basis during the first half of the twentieth century.

When Fergus Falls was fully open, it included an operating room and full-time dentist. 150 surgeries were carried out in the biennium ending in 1922, and innoculations of the typhoid vaccine were given to 5,200 patients.

Dental care, however, was limited in some facilities. Faribault employed a part-time dentist until 1938, and the dental office in Cambridge was open only two days a week, despite a patient population of over 2,400.[1] The Cambridge dental office was staffed by one full-time dentist, working six days a week for $1,800 a year, and "a very capable bright patient who assists him in his work."[2]

In 1914, eighteen hundred patients and employees at Fergus Falls were given anti-typhoid vaccinations. The rationale behind the vaccinations was that, "Prior to the use of prophylactic vaccine we not infrequently had employes sick with typhoid fever, but since its use we have had no employes sick with the disease, and consequently, there has been no loss of their service to the state."[3]

Willmar underwent a change, in 1936, from a custodial model to providing active hospital treatment. A laboratory was developed and a dental unit opened. Patients were reclassified and regrouped.[4]

A card index system for all patients was developed and all the male patients and some females were given physical exams. There was no record of these patients having had any previous physicals since entering the hospital.[5] Despite having had a dentist, the need for providing additional dental care on the wards was evident. The superintendent stated that oral hygiene, especially among the deteriorated patients, was at a low ebb. Gingivitis was found almost universally. A large number of patients needed treatment for mouth infections caused by Vincent's organisms. The treatment was tedious and the results were not satisfactory.[6]

Smallpox inoculations were added to the typhoid vaccines given to new patients after an outbreak of smallpox at St. Peter in 1937. They also experienced an epidemic of dysentery in one building, contributing to the death of several elderly patients.[7]

In an example of the lack of preventative medical care, when all the patients at Willmar were tested in 1943, seventy-two percent were found to have pin worms. In some cottages, the rate was ninety-six percent.[8]

By mid-century, medical care varied between excellent and very limited across the hospitals. Rochester's proximity to the Mayo Clinic enabled them to provide more specialized care. Providing services without charging the state or patients, Mayo doctors performed 588 surgeries in 1948.[9] St. Peter utilized the surgical services of doctors from the Mankato Clinic, who performed twenty-one surgeries during 1936-38.[10]

Anoka, on the other hand, had specialists available only twice a month. In 1949, there was no money available, and the use of consultants had to be discontinued.[11] Other hospitals had to call around to neighboring communities to find an available doctor when the need arose.

The other side of Mayo's involvement with the Rochester State hospital was research. The effects of unilateral adrenalectomy and alterations in the autonomic nervous system following lobotomy were studied in 1948. Micro electrodes were placed deep in patient's brains during lobotomies and left there for several weeks to study electrical potentials in 1952. Patients were said to be up and about with the electrodes in place with no discomfort.[12] Numerous drugs were studied and a number of articles published from these studies.

Other state hospitals lacked doctors, support personnel, equipment and supplies. There were a total of twenty-nine physicians in the entire state hospital system in December of 1947 for over 10,000 patients. Six additional positions were unfilled. Ratios ranged from one physician for 236 patients, up to one for 698.[13] However, even these numbers are deceiving, for one of these physician's positions at each hospital was held by the superintendent. While they had medical responsibilities, most of their time was taken up with administrative duties.

Low salaries made it difficult to recruit staff. Doctors were paid from $397 to $457 per month in 1948, with some deductions if they roomed and boarded on the hospital grounds. Doctors' families lived in as few as two rooms with an adjoining bath.[14]

Some medical positions went unfilled, so the clinical medicine provided was limited. At Anoka, there were 560 patients per doctor and a lack of equipment needed for diagnosis.[15]

Medical care was in such short supply that diabetic ulcers at Anoka went untreated.[16] In a similar manner, the response to a case of stomach cancer was to allow the family to take the patient home. A patient needing cataract surgery could get it at the university, but only if the family paid. A family became upset because their relative's sarcoma of the eye was causing a lot of pain. The family agreed to pay seventy-five dollars for an operation.[17] There wasn't even money in the budget to pay for patients' glasses. An inspector at Anoka commented that a patient who was working in the sewing room had gone for over a year with the right lens of her glasses broken and tied on with a string.[18]

Nurses were also in short supply, with a total of eighty-two employed system-wide in December 1947. The state had allocated 115 positions. St. Peter had its full compliment of twenty-six, while Willmar had only four of twelve, and two other hospitals were missing fifty percent of their nursing staff. Nurses in some hospitals lived above or adjacent to patient wards in spaces that were poorly heated and ventilated. Superintendents complained about the poor quality of the furnishings they could provide for nurses' rooms. Nursing ratios varied from 1:73 to 1:351.[19]

When you consider the wide range of medical tasks performed by nurses, the numbers demonstrate an impossibility. It should be remembered that nurses ran wards, and thus much of their time was also tied up with paperwork and administrative tasks.

Not only the staff but the facilities available for sick patients were inadequate. In Anoka, ill patients were cared for on the second floor of a cottage that had no elevator, so they had to be carried up and down the stairs in stretchers. With only a few small rooms available, dying patients were housed in a large ward. Other bedridden patients were upset when deaths occurred in their midst. The only sinks available for nurses or doctors to wash their hands were in a large patient bathroom. The area used by the dentist was on the same floor and had water available only in the spit bowl attached to the dental chair.[20]

In addition to being one of the few doctors at the hospital—and perhaps the only one with psychiatric training—superintendents had to deal with a myriad of administrative details. Superintendents' files are filled with letters flowing back and forth discussing whether the state or county should pay, and how much, to repair the hospital roads. They were involved in arranging the transfer of stud boars and exchanging recipes for 180 pounds of meatloaf and 100 loaves of bread.

Examples of the petty paperwork that occupied superintendents includes the time when the superintendent of the School for the Deaf was informed that he had made an error in his December 1903 statement of cash receipts. The State Auditor and State Treasurer agreed that he had to repay the money from his own pocket. All these august individuals were consulted and letters sent back and forth over the weighty matter of ten cents.[21]

It would be tempting to blame these conditions on the hospitals. The Moose Lake superintendent wrote to the Cambridge superintendent in June of 1941 asking for support. He had traveled over 1,000 miles over a period of months attempting to recruit physicians. He suggested approaching the Civil Service Board to get salaries increased. When the Hastings superintendent heard that another hospital had found a way to pay for patients' glasses, he wrote to inquire what fund they had used.[22]

Hospital conditions weren't what the superintendents chose, but the best they could provide.

NOTES

1. *Minnesota School for Feeble-Minded and Colony for Epileptics Farbault and Colony for Epileptics Cambridge,* June 30, 1938, p. 10.
2. Letter, Dr. McBroom to Dr. Enberg, March 22, 1941.
3. *Seventh Biennial Report to the State Board of Control,* July 31, 1914, p. 136.
4. *Biennial Report Of the Institutions for the Insane of the State Board of Control of*

Minnesota, June 30, 1936, p. 18.

5. *Biennial Report Of the Institutions for the Insane of the State Board of Control of Minnesota,* June 30, 1936, p. 17.

6. *Biennial Report Of the Institutions for the Insane of the State Board of Control of Minnesota,* June 30, 1936, p. 17.

7. *Biennial Report Of the Hospitals for the Insane of Minnesota,* June 30, 1938, p. 41.

8. Willmar State Hospital, *Biennial Report,* June 30, 1943.

9. Rochester State Hospital, *Biennial Report,* 1948.

10. *Biennial Report Of the Hospitals for the Insane of Minnesota,* June 30, 1938, p. 42.

11. Anoka staff conference minutes, 1949.

12. Minnesota State Institutions, *Rochester State Hospital Biennial Report,* 1954.

13. *Minnesota Unitarian Conference. Committee on State Hospitals for the Mentally Ill,* Unitarian Report, 1948.

14. Minneapolis *Tribune,* May 14, 1948, p. 8.

15. Anoka State Hospital, *Progress Report,* 1950.

16. Anoka staff conference minutes, 1947.

17. Anoka staff conference minutes, 1948 .

18. Visitation Record, Anoka State Hospital July 10, 1945, Social Security Department.

19. Unitarian Report, 1948.

20. Control Board,"Recommendations, Anoka," 1946.

21. Letter, Board of Control to J. Tate, Superintendent, January 30, 1904, Faribault School for the Deaf letters.

22. Cambridge, correspondence.

Chapter Fifteen

Death

DURING ITS FIRST YEARS, ST. PETER RECORDED the causes of patient deaths. Below is a table from the 1888 report.

Cause	Men	Women
Apoplexy	18	7
Abcess of brain	0	1
Assault by patient	3	2
Anasarca	3	1
Ascites	1	0
Asthenia	13	6
Addidson's Disease	1	0
Bright's Disease	1	1
Cancer	3	0
Cholera morbus	1	0
Carbuncle	1	0
Congestion of lungs	7	3
Cirrhosis of liver	0	1
Cerebral congestion	1	0
Continued fever	0	2
Diarrhea	9	10
Drowning	1	1
Dysentery	1	1
Diabetes	2	0
Exhaustion from mania	32	44
Exhaustion from melancholia	14	6

Enteritis, acute	4	2
Epilepsy	50	41
Erysipelas	6	3
Exposure	0	2
Embolism	0	2
Endocarditis	1	0
Gangrene	0	1
Hamoptisis	1	0
Hernia (incarcerated)	1	0
Hemorrage, accidental	1	0
Heart Disease	10	1
Gastroenteritis	0	1
Inflammation throat	1	0
Intestinal obstruction	0	1
Killed by cars	1	0
Measles	1	0
Marasmus	65	67
Missing (burned)	24	0
Meningitis	5	2
Old age	15	8
Organic brain disease	4	2
Occlusion of hepatic duct	0	1
Phthisis	54	52
Paralysis	15	21
Pneumonia	18	11
Pericarditis	1	1
Peritonitis	3	1
Pleurisy	1	0
Progressive Paralysis	27	0
Rheumatism	1	1

Scrofulosis	1	0
Suicide	6	4
Shock from burn	0	1
Secondary hemorrage	0	1
Spedalsked	0	1
Softening of brain	5	3
Senile Dementia	7	0
Syphilis	2	0
Typhomania	10	14
Typhoid fever	2	4
Thrombosis of heart	2	3
Variola	4	0

Some of the high number of deaths reflect the patient population. Marasmus—or a wasting associated with senility—would be expected among aged patients admitted because they had become confused. Epilepsy was a common reason for sending someone to a state hospital.

Syphilis is noted in only two instances. The twenty-seven cases of progressive paralysis in men raise the possibility that syphilis was more common than the doctors then realized. In future years, syphilis would become a significant percentage of hospital admission diagnoses.

Deaths due to exhaustion from mania would continue in state hospitals until the advent of modern drugs. They illustrate the strength of some mental disorders and the challenges staff faced in attempting to keep patients calm. Exhaustion from melancholia is more difficult for us to understand. Were patients so unhappy that they curled up on their beds and died?

The twenty-four deaths from burning occurred during the fire in the men's wing at St. Peter in 1880.

The dangers present in the hospital can be seen in the five deaths caused by other patients. A lack of fences at the hospital may have contributed to the two drownings and a car accident. Death by violence wasn't confined to hospitals for the insane—the combined report for Faribault and Cambridge lists four deaths during 1935-1936 by violence other than suicide.[1]

A lack of staff and treatment options meant that patients continued to kill each other for most of the years in which state hospitals operated. An eighty-two-year-old Anoka patient died from a fractured skull in 1948, three days after he was pushed by another. When relatives asked for an investigation, the superintendent reported to the governor that at the time of the incident, two attendants had been caring for 200 patients. He pointed out that they averaged one-point-three attendants per 100 patients, but that staff had to be pulled for lawn and garden details, stretcher bearers, delivering ice and taking patients to appointments in Anoka. [2]

The prevalence of Phthisis (TB) among patients who were often crowded into wards was recorded from state hospitals earliest days, but wouldn't be dealt with until the 1930s. Death was commonplace in the state hospitals, especially those that housed chronic patients. Two hundred deaths were recorded at Anoka during the 1950 biennium.

BURIAL

WHEN A PATIENT AT FARIBAULT DIED, the family was notified and told that they could have the body transported at their own expense. If they preferred, a service could be held at the hospital chapel with a minister from the families' religion, and the body buried in the hospital cemetery.[3]

A rotation was established among local funeral homes to equally distribute services paid for by the state. Funeral homes were paid seventy-two dollars in 1955—and ten dollars more if a Catholic priest officiated. They were to provide a pine casket covered in gray material and with removable liner and handles; hearse; embalming, cosmetizing and dressing the remains; transporting parents; and acknowledgement cards.[4]

There was no cost for a headstone. State law required that graves in state institution cemeteries, "shall be indicated by an appropriate marker of permanent nature for identification purposes."[5] This was accomplished by filling a coffee can with cement and pressing the patient's hospital number into the top.

Ministers and priests conducted funerals at St. Peter. In the winter, however, they didn't accompany the bodies up to the hospital cemetery, leaving that to the grounds crew. In one case, the crew had a horse already hitched to a manure spreader, so that was used to transport a patient's body.[6]

Under the provisions of the State Anatomical Act, bodies unclaimed after thirty-six hours were sent to medical colleges for anatomical study. The deans of the medical schools appointed members to the State Anatomical Committee, who apportioned the bodies between the various educational institutions. The Minnesota statute regarding the disposal of bodies from the state hospitals reads, "The remains of any such body, after it has answered the purposes, shall be decently buried in a public cemetery and the expense of transporting and burying such body shall be borne by the college receiving the same."[7] In the first six months of 1922, three bodies were sent from Faribault to the Medical School at the University of Minnesota "for burial."[8]

In 1930, the State Board of Control authorized the Ah-Gwah-Ching tuberculosis sanitarium to buy land for a cemetery ". . . to provide for the burial of patients, provided the bodies are not desired by the University Hospital."[9] This would seem to have given the university a routine claim to bodies from the sanitarium. Willmar delivered three bodies to the State Anatomical Board during the biennium ending June 1938.[10]

The procedure when a body was unclaimed at Faribault in the fall of 1958 included informing the head of the Department of Anatomy at the University of Minnesota, who chaired the State Anatomical Committee. He was told the patient's name and transportation arrangements were made, with costs paid by the committee. A receipt for the body was placed in the patient's file at Faribault.[11]

The dean of the University of Minnesota medical school complained in 1950 about the lack of cooperation from many of the state hospitals, resulting in a shortage of cadavers for dissection. Four medial students had to share a cadaver, instead of the preferred two. He pointed out that the university provided services to the state institutions, and said that the Medical School at the University of Indiana obtained virtually all its anatomical material from state institutions.[12]

The chair of the state Anatomical Committee supported the university's efforts by informing the superintendent at Faribault that bodies were not to be sent to Mayo. They were permitted to use unclaimed bodies only from Olmsted County.[13]

Beginning in 1994, a group called Remembering with Dignity began work to place a headstone on every unmarked state hospital grave. That laudatory effort can never encompass all of those whose bodies rest in anonymous sites, for the final resting places of patients whose bodies were unclaimed and were sent to medical schools is unknown.

The situation is further complicated in the Hastings State Hospital cemetery, because it's not clear where all the people buried there came from. The Homeless Men's Camp in Savage, Minnesota, had no burial space, and asked for permission to use the Hastings State Hospital cemetery. They were granted permission in 1941. Expenses had to be borne by the homeless camp, and the hospital provided a burial service.[14]

NOTES

1. *Minnesota School for Feeble-Minded and Colony for Epileptics Farbault and Colony for Epileptics Cambridge,* June 30, 1936.
2. Governor Youndahl's records, public institutions.
3. Letter M. Enberg to Commissioner of Mental Health. Faribault, superintendent correspondence, August 16, 1950.
4. Faribault State School and Hospital, Death and Burial Records, March 1955.
5. Letter, M Teslow Division of Public Institutions to E. Enberg, May 5, 1952, Faribault superintendent subject files—letters.
6. R.L. staff interviews. Archives at St. Peter State Hospital museum.
7. Faribault, superintendent correspondence, unclaimed bodies citing Minnesota stature 145.14.
8. Faribault State School and Hospital, Death and Burial Records.
9. Control Board minutes, Oct 6, 1930.
10. Willmar State Hospital, *Biennial Report,* June 30, 1938.
11. Letter, E. Enberg to Dr. Smith, Clinical Director, Faribault superintendent correspondence, unclaimed bodies.
12. Letter, Diehl, Harold—Dean University Medical School—to Dr. Ralph Rossen, Commissioner of Mental Health, December 12, 1950. www.mnddc.org/past.
13. Boyden, E.A. Chairman, State Anatomical Committee to Superintendent School for Feeble-Minded, December 4, 1950. www.mnddc.org/past.
14. Letter, Hastings Superintendent to Carl Swanson, January 25, 1941, Public Welfare Correspondence, Hastings.

Chapter Sixteen
Psychiatric Treatment Attempts

Hospital superintendents and doctors did what they could to alleviate patients' psychiatric problems. There were no cures available, and few interventions could provide long-term improvement. As treatments surfaced, they were implemented.

In the 1800s, treatments included lots of milk, good food, activities and bed rest. Fergus Falls kept people in bed with sheets. St. Peter used "cribs" which looked much like oversized coffins. Straw was put in the bottom, patients lay down inside, and a wooden screen was placed over the top. Dorthea Dix, the nurse famous for her care of the mentally ill and ministrations during the civil war, visited St. Peter in 1874, and criticized the hospital for using cribs too often.

The end stages of syphilis could cause brain dysfunction. Labeled a form of insanity, it was a common cause for admission to state hospitals. An early treatment for syphilis utilized IV neoarsphenamine and mercury. There was no improvement in a good many cases, but certain patients distinctly benefited and made the treatment well worth carrying out.[1]

After World War I, Austrian psychiatrist Julius Wagner-Jaruegg injected malaria-infected blood into a patient with syphilis. The patient markedly improved. It was thought that the high fever killed some of the spirochete that were known to cause syphilis. He was awarded the Nobel Prize in medicine in 1927 for his work.[2]

The malaria treatment was carried out at Rochester State Hospital in collaboration with the Mayo Clinic. Beginning in 1929, patients were injected with the blood of patients who had malaria. Careful records were kept of the onset of the first chill and subsequent fevers. Treatments were first carried out at St. Mary's Hospital, and later at the state hospital.[3] The malaria treatment was found to be successful in Rochester. During the biennium ending in 1930, sixty-seven patients were treated with malaria. Of these patients, eleven recovered and went home, ten died from various causes during the treatment, twenty remained unimproved, and twenty-two showed improvement of varying degrees. Of the four manic patients given the treatment, three remained unimproved and one recovered mentally and physically and returned home.[4] As odd and risky as this sounds now, waiting until the treatment had been recognized with a Nobel Prize represented a conservative, careful approach.

Another kind of treatment attempt occurred at Willmar, where inebriate patients were routinely given spinal drainages to relieve the increased pressure caused by alcoholism.[5]

Hastings State Hospital developed a method of improving patient behavior in the late 1930s. They began utilizing a behavior system for patients. Those who mistreated other patients or staff lost the privilege of attending movies or parties and could not eat in the dining room. They had to participate in exercise twice a day, and spend time on a bench. Within six months, Hastings had reduced the number of patients in restraints from fifty-five to four, and two of these who remained in restraints were patients who attempted to injure themselves. The type of restraint used was also reduced, from camisoles to wristlets and sheets. They were also able to decrease the use of barbiturates. These results were discussed with other superintendents and the director of Public Institutions in 1940.[6]

These dramatic improvements, using behavior techniques only, were achieved before the advent of much more intrusive and dangerous interventions that became common throughout the Minnesota state hospital system in the next fifteen years. The record doesn't say why this benign approach, well documented for over a year at Hastings, wasn't adopted by the other hospitals. The program took some time—the Hastings superintendent said staff and patients had initially adjusted over a six-month period. It would have required a good deal of staff training. Perhaps because it didn't produce immediate results, or because it ran against the contemporary excitement generated by modern treatments, it was ignored by the other state hospitals.

One of history's ironies is that B.F. Skinner had recently come to the University of Minnesota. The man who would later become a pioneer of behavioral programming was living less than an hour away from an institution that had on its own developed an effective behavior program.

What was not discussed by anyone at Hastings was the radical assumption that psychiatric patients could learn to control much of their behavior, given appropriate incentives. Perhaps it was the lack of a theoretical framework that caused the behavioral treatment to be considered unimportant. Behavior programming would have had to be directed by the hospital physicians. It was not a pill, a surgery or individual treatment. This may have put it outside the bounds of what was considered medical intervention.

I have relegated Hasting's successful behavior program to the place it played in Minnesota state hospital history—lumping it with what were considered crude early treatment attempts. Had it been widely adopted within the same state hospital system where it had been shown to work, a great deal of suffering and damage inflicted on patients could have been avoided.

NOTES

1. *Biennial Report Hospitals and asylums for the Insane Minnesota*, June 30, 1922, p. 18.
2. Robert Whitaker. *Mad in America*, Basic Books, New York, 2002, p. 83.
3. Rochester State Hospital, special clinical records.
4. *Biennial Report Hospitals and asylums for the Insane Minnesota*, June 30, 1930, p. 25.
5. *Biennial Report Of the Institutions for the Insane of the State Board of Control of Minnesota*, June 30, 1936, p. 17.
6. Letter, Hastings Superintendent to Carl Swanson, December 10, 1940, Public Welfare Correspondence, Hastings.

CHAPTER SEVENTEEN
AGRESSIVE TREATMENT APPROACHES

PSYCHIATRY TURNED AWAY FROM WAREHOUSING PATIENTS to seeking cures in the 1940s. The first major goal was producing a calming effect. Even if it lasted for only twenty-four hours, bringing a patient down from an agitated or aggressive state was beneficial to them and the ward.

Hydrotherapy was one early method, carried out by placing patients in a warm bath for up to twelve hours. Another version wrapped patients in a warm wet sheet and then two blankets. This was designed to provide a warm medium. Patients might be left in the blankets overnight.[1] Some Minnesota state hospitals had hydrotherapy equipment, but lacked trained staff to use them.[2]

Insulin therapy was used by the British during World War II and made its way to the United States. In this method, patients were put into a coma deep enough that epileptic fits might occur, though staff attempted to avoid setting off a seizure because patients' backs could break. Care was needed to get the patient out of their coma before too long, or it could become irreversible. To end the coma, glucose was given via naso-gastric tube. The tubes were difficult to insert during comas, and occasionally were inserted into lungs.[3] The records of Rochester State Hospital list one death from insulin shock.[4]

Willmar developed a new method of delivering insulin via IV, instead of intramuscular injections. Convulsions could be produced with greater regularity and the time between the injection and coma was reduced.[5]

Protocols on how to carry out insulin treatment differed widely between hospitals. For example, some protocols called for using insulin to produce a twenty-minute coma six days a week for six to ten weeks,[6] and while Willmar deliberately put patients into convulsions,[7] St. Peter carefully observed patients to prevent them from convulsing.[8] What type of patient would benefit from the insulin treatment was also not clear. St. Peter first used the treatment on two women with dementia praecox.[9]

The benefits of insulin were noted in the first year at St. Peter. A male patient was described as "aggressive, pugnacious and quite threatening." After treatment, doctors wrote, "he is very often pleasant and affable for quite extended periods of time and no longer requires restraint. In fact, his folks have even suggested that he is better than he was before he became ill."[10]

It was noted on autopsies that insulin comas caused brain damage, in proportion to the number of treatments that had been given. A theory was developed that damaging an insane brain was therapeutic. Psychotic symptoms were reduced because higher cognitive and emotional functions had been reduced.[11] This "decortation" theory supported the development of subsequent treatments. It sounds very odd to us today to embark on a treatment regime with the stated goal: "I'm going to stop you from behaving oddly by damaging your brain sufficiently that you will not be capable of those behaviors." With no other way of improving patients' functioning, this was seen as an appropriate rationale. They would not be highly intelligent, fully functioning individuals, but neither would they be screaming, weeping, or destroying their environment. Surely, this was an improvement.

Another treatment method was administering Metrazol, a drug that induced explosive seizures. The New York State Psychiatric Institute reported that forty-three percent of patients treated with Metrazol suffered spinal fractures. It could also cause hemorrhages in the brain, lungs, kidneys and spleen. Patients were dazed, friendly and cooperative for some time afterward.[12] St. Peter reported that there was a short interval after Metrazol was given that patients felt they were going to die. As a consequence, patients hated and feared the treatments.[13, 14] It was used on a limited basis at Rochester and St. Peter before being discontinued in favor of electroconvulsive therapy (ECT), which didn't elicit the same amount of fear in patients.[15]

ECT became quite popular. It was noted that schizophrenic epileptic patients seemed better after a seizure. Autopsies of patients with dementia and epilepsy showed opposite glia cell counts in the brain. A theory of antagonism was developed, on the premise that one disease was the antagonist of the other. Thus, inducing seizures would reduce mental illness.

ECT was administered by placing electrodes on the head, and staff applied sufficient electricity to induce a seizure. These seizures could lead to broken limbs, crushed vertebrae, dislocated jaws and chronic neck pain. After 1950, muscle relaxants were administered just prior to the electrodes being placed so that only the patient's facial muscles twitched. This eliminated injuries and reduced patients' fear of the treatment.

Use of ECT at Rochester peaked at 23,317 treatments in 1952. They were delivered to 590 patients, an average of almost forty per patient. As many as sixty percent of patients with involutional psychosis recovered after two or three months with the use of ECT.[16] Patients at Willmar were given as many as ten shocks in one session.[17]

A new way of inducing seizures was tried at Hastings in 1941. Termed a shock treatment, anoxic treatments limited oxygen to the brain by compressing the carotid arteries until a moderate degree of clonic spasm was produced. Patients felt little and had no recollection of what took place. Several doctors from the Mayo Clinic as well as the director of the State Mental Health Unit traveled to Hastings for a demonstration. The director told Carl Swanson that,

> The spasms produced were not severe and the treatment was under control at all times. By removing the pressure, consciousness returned almost immediately. Following the demonstration we held a conference relative to the merits and disadvantages of the experiment involved and decided it was worth continuing until further data could be compiled. Also recommended a few changes in the mechanical set-up.[18]

In what would be considered a counterintuitive treatment by neurologists today, the aggressive behavior of an epileptic teenager at Faribault was addressed by giving her frequent electronic treatments. Her behavior improved, but she continued to break eyeglasses of patients and staff and was recommended for a lobotomy by the medical superintendent at Rochester State Hospital.[19]

Patients were often calm for twenty-four hours after an ECT session. In some cases—particularly paranoia and depression—longer term benefits were noted. Prior to the use of muscle relaxants, patients were anxious and fearful about subsequent ECT sessions. It required a lot of people and effort to hold patients down while they seizured. In some cases, patients waiting their turn for a treatment assisted. It's difficult to imagine helping hold a patient down while he or she went into a full-blown seizure, knowing that it was soon going to be their own turn to get on the table. ECT was given to a wide variety of patients, including those with dementia.

Not content with the short term effects of the treatments at hand, state hospitals began experimenting with combining treatments.

A number of experiments were carried out at Willmar involving electroshock therapy during the 1943 biennium.[20] In multiple electroshock therapy, patients were given as many as ten electric shocks during a single convulsion. Coramine was given intravenously just prior to the electroshock treatment. Later, an equal amount of distilled water was given, after the maximum effect of the coramine was obtained.

Metrazol was tried in place of the coramine and was found to be far more effective. The patient was given enough Metrazol to induce a convulsion. When the convulsion began, the electroshock treatment was given.

Tolserol and Dilantin, separately and together, were tried in order to reduce the severity of convulsions. Curare and synthetic Syncuring were also used for this purpose. Other drugs tried in combination with electroshock treatment included sodium amythal, atropine, codeine, seconal and nembutal. Atropine was then routinely used because it helped restore respiration and circulation. Codeine combined with seconal or numbutal was effective in reducing patients' fear of electroshock treatments. Music was played in the treatment and recovery rooms, in another attempt to calm patients.[21] Rochester experimented as well, putting patients into an insulin coma, and then administering ECT.

These weren't the first examples of treatment experiments being carried out on Minnesota State Hospital patients. Rattlesnake venom was used as an experimental treatment for epilepsy in Faribault in 1911. Results weren't clear but reports at the time stated that "no harm has been done." At the time the inspectors visited, it had not yet been tried on women.[22] Another experimental treatment occurred at Campbridge in 1929, in an attempt to reduce seizures, but the results were "not gratifying" and it was discontinued. [23]

These experiments were not the work of some crackpot doctors secretly using state hospital patients as guinea pigs. Rather, the results were proudly reported to the state central office and seemed to reflect best medical practice at the time. This also means that the highest levels of state government were comfortable with what was being done.

Today's experimental protocols demand that great measures be taken to protect patients' safety and rights. The milieu that existed in 1940s state hospitals was utterly bleak. For fifty years, the vast majority of patients deteriorated until they died. Here was a chance that modern medicine could cure some of them enough to be discharged. The ethical dictum—cause no harm—was loosened, because patients were seen as having very little to lose. Thus, in the face of hopelessness, efforts to provide hope made sense.

LOBOTOMIES

BY 1948, APPROXIMATELY 5,000 PATIENTS had been given pre-frontal lobotomies in the United States. Walter Freeman, the chief proponent of lobotomies, theorized that disrupting connections to the thalamus blunted patients' emotional responses.[24] He stated that lobotomies resulted in patients displaying the Boy Scout virtues in reverse. They showed a lack of trustworthiness, loyalty, helpfulness, friendliness, courtesy, kindness, obedience, cheerfulness, thriftiness, bravery, cleanliness and reverence.[25]

Few controlled studies were conducted to document the effects. A Swedish investigator studied thirty-two post-lobotomy patients. Family members stated that their relative had "lost their soul." He described patients who felt no real happiness or sorrow, their thinking was concrete, they perseverated, they had lost their sense of the value of money, and had little interest in everyday happenings. He suggested developing a method of a partial lobectomy that avoided these problems, and he was reluctant to operate on non-psychotic patients.[26]

Willmar performed forty-six lobotomies between January 1941 and June 1943, on chronic patients who were destructive, violent and untidy. Nine were subsequently discharged or paroled while many others improved to the point that they could work and have liberty of the grounds. At the time, it was written, "the procedure is comparatively new and the indications are, as yet, not sharply delineated." Three patients were given second bilateral lobotomies.[27] The lobotomy program was begun, despite not knowing which patients it would help.

State laws allowed hospital superintendents to authorize necessary surgeries on patients when the consent of a guardian could not be obtained. The Minnesota Attorney General's office ruled in September of 1947 that lobotomies were included because they could be considered necessary for mental health.[28] This ruling opened the door to more lobotomies by getting around the problem of unresponsive families.

Anoka sent patients to the university for lobotomies. Nurses complained that some patients regressed and lost bladder control after their lobotomy and that incisions became infected.[29] Some other state hospitals could offer only twenty-five dollars per operation, and had difficulty recruiting doctors to conduct the surgery.[30]

Hastings was able to perform lobotomies, and patients were sent there from other hospitals. The report of a visit by the head of the State Mental Health Unit was forwarded to the governor. It included: "Doctor Patterson is pleased with the prospect of participating in a psychosurgery program which is in prospect at the Hastings State Hospital. Details of the plan have yet to be worked out but I believe it will be a worth-while venture even though the chronically mentally ill patient is not the most favorable one for operation so far as 'cure' is concerned."[31] That's a rather startling statement, shared at the highest levels of state government. Lobotomies were going to be carried out on chronic patients, despite the lack of evidence that they would produce a cure.

Forty-three percent of the Hastings lobotomy patients showed moderate to marked improvement after surgery. (The outcomes for the other fifty-seven percent weren't noted.) Walter Freeman visited Minnesota in 1949 and performed several icepick lobotomies at Hastings State Hospital.[32]

Collaboration with the Mayo Clinic enabled the Rochester State Hospital to carry out lobotomies. By 1954, 493 had been performed. Prior to 1952, only thirty-seven-point-seven percent of lobotomized patients were able to be discharged. This rate climbed to an anticipated sixty-five percent after the surgery was modified.[33]

LOBOTOMIES AND THE FEEBLE-MINDED

LOBOTOMIES WERE ALSO CARRIED OUT ON mentally deficient patients from Faribault State Hospital. The surgeries used were pre-frontal lobotomies—three of them bilateral—performed at the Hastings, Sandstone and Rochester State Hospitals, and one at the Mayo Clinic. In two cases, patients had second lobotomies, one of which was after an initial bilateral lobotomy. Several patients were noted to have epilepsy prior to the operations.

Patients IQs ranged from sixty-five to as low as twenty-six and eleven. Several were said to be untestable, and one too low to rate. The mental status on one male wasn't taken. All the patients were aggressive to themselves or others. The Faribault superintendent saw them as more tractable, contented and easier to manage and said he would be recommending others for the same procedure.[34]

The surgery was not without risk. Aggressive, mentally deficient patients were not always cooperative, and serious post-operative problems could developed after the lobotomy. Faribault's superintentent wrote of one patient: "She had developed a bad habit of picking her operative incision and has in this way prevented it in healing properly. At the present time there is still some difficulty with the site which she has irritated continually and has been necessary to employ mittens on her hands to keep her from digging at the operation."[35]

As late as 1965, five Faribault inmates were considered for lobotomies. The list included a seventeen-year-old with an IQ of thirty who had already had one lobotomy performed at Rochester State Hospital when he was fifteen, with no improvement in behavior.[36] Repeatedly lobotomizing a mentally impaired teenager marks a low point in the history of Minnesota lobotomies.

The operations made them easier to handle in the institutions, but no mention was made of the possibility of discharging any feeble-minded patients. Much of the rational for lobotomies—that they would benefit the patient—don't seem to apply here. Putting the best spin on the outcomes, it could be argued that patients were less agitated. Does that mean they were happier? It could also be argued that these surgeries were for the benefit of the institution, not the individuals whose brains got scrambled.

Many of these treatments seem ineffectual and barbaric to us now. In 1950, hospital superintendents were thrilled that increased funding would allow them to provide these treatments to more patients. They were moving from hopelessness—physical or chemical restraint—to hope.

NOTES

1. Simon Baruch, MD. *Hydrotherapy*, William Wood & Co, NY, 1948.
2. Minneapolis *Tribune*, May 17, p.1.
3. P.D. Laing, Wisdon. *Madness and Folly*, M.C. Graw Hill Book Co, New York, 1985, p. 90.
4. Rochester State Hospital, patient register 1947-48.
5. Willmar State Hospital, *Biennial Report*, June 30, 1938.
6. Hugh Freeman, *Century of Psychiatry*, Harcourt Publishers, 1999.
7. Willmar State Hospital, *Biennial Report*, June 30, 1938.
8. *Insulin Shock Therapy*, St. Peter Regional Treatment Center.
9. Monthly report, St. Peter SH, January 1937, St. Peter SH Collection, Archives Minnesota State University, Mankato.
10. Monthly report, St. Peter SH, March 1937, St. Peter SH Collection, Archives Minnesota State University, Mankato.
11. *Mad in America*, pp. 89, 99.
12. *Ibid.*, p. 95.
13. *A History of Psychiatry*, p. 216.
14. Monthly report, St. Peter SH, January 1944, St. Peter SH Collection, Archives Minnesota State University, Mankato.
15. Rochester State Hospital, *Biennial Report*, 1940.
16. Rochester, *Biennial Report*, 1952.
17. Letter, E. McBroom to Carl Swanson, December 1, 1941, Public Welfare Correspondence, Hastings.
18. Faribault Superintendent correspondence, lobotomy file, September 15, 1950.
19. *Ibid.*

20. Willmar State Hospital, *Biennial Report*, June 30, 1943.
21. *Ibid.*
22. Visitors Report, October 15, 1911. Faribault—unbound records. Reports of Inspections.
23. Letter, Dr. McBroom to Gillette Hospital, February 1, 1934, Cambridge correspondence.
24. Jack el Hai. *The Lobotomist*, Wiley & Sons, New Jersey, p. 165.
25. *The Lobotomist*, p. 197.
26. *Research on Prefrontal lobotomy*, Group for the Advancement of Psychiatry, Topeka, June 1948, p. 1.
27. Willmar State Hospital, *Biennial Report*, June 30, 1943.
28. Public Welfare Department, Carl Swanson, correspondence, September 25, 1947.
29. Anoka staff conference minutes, 1948.
30. Willmar State Hospital, *Biennial Report*, 1948.
31. Letter to Governor Youngdahl from Carl Jackson. Governor Youngdahl.
32. Office of Commissioner of Mental Health, *13th Biennial Report*, 1950.
33. Rochester, *Biennial Report*, 1954.
34. Letter E. Enberg to L Yepson Director Mental Deficiency, New Jersey July 18, 1952. Faribault State Hospital & School Superintendent subject files, lobotomy.
35. Faribault, Superintendent correspondence, lobotomies, April 3, 1963.
36. Faribault, Superintendent correspondence, lobotomies, Memo to Dr. Smith February 1, 1965.

CHAPTER EIGHTEEN
THE REFORM MOVEMENT

A FEW VOICES BEGAN SPEAKING OUT as early as the 1930s that simply warehousing patients made little sense—from either a humane or an economic viewpoint. Eugenic principals came into disrepute when the end of World War II revealed the extent of Nazi atrocities. Operating genetic jails no longer made any sense. Despite their limited success, aggressive psychiatric treatments created an orientation that patients could—and should—be helped.

The Willmar superintendent, speaking courageously in his 1938 Biennial Report said, "It is demonstrated here as well as other places, that with intensive treatment many of these individuals recover and leave the hospitals. . . . It is further recommended that the social service work be conducted directly from the hospital. This would make placement of the patient easier and the supervision after he leaves the hospital better."[1]

Although his comments elicited little change in the system, he was more explicit five years later, in his 1943 Biennial Report. In it, he wrote,

> It is a well-known fact that more intensive and more individualized treatment definitely shortens the period of hospitalization. While this does not reduce the per capita cost, it does lower the number of patients that must be housed and provided for. Many of the patients recover or improve in proportion to the amount of individual attention given them. It is discouraging to realize that the recovery of many patients is prevented or retarded due to lack of personnel and equipment. Therefore, an increase in personnel is advocated from an economic as well as from a humanitarian point of view."[2]

Major construction projects for a number of state hospitals were approved in 1945 and 1947, including eight units for senile patients, three receiving units and a recreation building.[3] The 1947 legislature also authorized the complete rebuilding of the Rochester State Hospital.[4]

In 1946, the Unitarian Conference of Minnesota authorized a committee to study the conditions in Minnesota state hospitals for the mentally ill. In 1947, Governor Youngdahl, a Republican, appointed the chairman of the Unitarian Committee to his Advisory Board on Mental Health.[5]

The Unitarian Committee financed a study for presentation to the governor. The governor's support for hospital reform can be seen in the collaboration between the governor's office and this outside, independent church group. It was a brave move for the governor to turn loose independent inspectors who would probably uncover conditions that could have large fiscal and political ramifications. It was made clear, in the fall of 1947, that state hospital superintendents were to cooperate with the inspectors coming to complete the Unitarian Report. They came with the governor's referral, and were to be extended every courtesy.[6]

The Unitarians hired Mr. Justin Reece and his wife to visit the state hospitals. During World War II, he was a conscientious objector and had worked in the Cleveland State Hospital.[7] He had been recommended to the Unitarians as the best qualified by the medical director of the National Mental Hygiene Society. He and his wife toured all the state mental hospitals in December 1947.

The Unitarian Report was delivered to the governor on April 26, 1948. It included findings of a lack of treatment and activities, overcrowding, poor clothing and personal hygiene, inadequate quantity and quality of food, overuse of restraints at several hospitals, few social work services to support patient release, and a lack of qualified staff. Their finding of an average cost of one dollar and five cents per day per patient was below the eleven dollar cost per day of general hospitals and the six dollars and fifty-two cents average for Veterans Administration mental hospitals.[8]

This dollar figure was attacked by a legislative research committee. They felt the value of agricultural products and clothing produced by the patients should be considered when calculating daily costs. They further felt that, "Minnesota mental patients are being given good treatment in nearly all cases, and the use of restraints is limited. The seven state hospitals are not terribly understaffed, as has been charged, because many patients are senile mental cases who require only custodial care, and not constant attendance."[9] Those who work in nursing homes today might dispute that statement about little care being needed for elderly patients.

The subcommittee displayed the courage of its convictions in the face of a sweeping exposé by the Minneapolis *Tribune*. Titled "Minnesota Bedlam," ten articles harshly criticized state hospital conditions. Several stories with headlines like "Medieval 'Restraints' Stay at State Mental Hospitals" were included. Photographs showed poorly dressed women with bowl haircuts restrained on benches in dark, bare day rooms.

These articles stated that the lack of treatment, combined with few activities, were said to lead to patient's deterioration. Meals were said to cost eight cents on average and were cold, unappetizing and monotonous. Food was eaten from tin dishes and bowl-like cups without handles.[10] These conditions were contrasted with the increased financial support and better care available in VA hospitals. The director of Minnesota's public institutions estimated that an additional six million dollars was needed for additional personnel and higher salaries.[11] Changes were called for in the commitment laws, particularly for children.

Governor Youngdahl actively supported the reform movement. He had been concerned about the treatment of people with mental illnesses since his time serving in municipal court. When he was elected governor, he toured many of the state hospitals and said, in a radio speech,

> I cannot tell you what anguish I have been through in visiting the hospitals which we maintain for these people—and seeing the lack of sufficient personnel and equipment.
>
> Here is what I have found in the state hospitals—the thing that hits one hard is going through—the herds of patients, lined up in chairs, sitting against walls, doing absolutely nothing, without even a clock or calendar to break the monotony of their existence. It means that there is little

> treatment going on—and it meant that patients are deteri-
> orating, many beyond hope of recovery.
>
> And then one goes through a few of the hospitals
> and sees patients tied up—in straps, and straight-jackets
> (called camisoles), and, in one, hospital chains.
>
> We pay men and women working with human beings
> less than one half of what industry pays people who do not
> have such responsibilities.[12]

The director of Public Institutions wrote to hospital superintendents on June 29, 1949, informing them that the governor had ordered that the use of restraints be abolished.[13] He wrote, "Keeping patients active is the secret to non-restraint. Progressive hospitals are placing more and more stress upon activity and thus are able to reduce restraint."[14]

The Minnesota Department of Social Security was aware of the issues, and supportive of the governor's efforts. Carl Jackson, the director of the Division of Public Institutions, provided a list of suggestions to the governor—many of which were adopted by the legislature.[15]

Governor Youngdahl organized a Governor's Council to recommend programming improvements. He then called together a second committee—the Governor's Citizens' Mental Health Committee. Fifty civic leaders—mainly lay persons—were given the task of mobilizing public opinion. Many counties organized local citizen's mental health committees. The rationale provided for the reform movement wasn't purely altruistic. It was felt that improved services could lead to more patients being cured and discharged from public support. The Governor said, "... I sincerely believe that the only true economy is to help the patient get well, and anything short of that is the false extravagance of penny pinching."[16]

A building program had recently begun for geriatric patients at several of the state hospitals. A powerful argument in favor of the reform movement was that it would remove the need for additional state hospital construction. The governor stated,

> I hope that after this building program is completed, we
> shall never have to build another custodial bed—that

through clinics we can keep many patients from going to state hospitals—that through active treatment we can so increase the number of discharges—the failure to do which, in the past, has been largely responsible for overcrowding—that except for replacements, our bed capacity will prove to be adequate."[17]

Opposition to the reform movement continued, with critics saying it made the state look bad, and that Minnesota was already doing well compared to other states.

Public opinion had swung strongly in favor of the reform, and the 1949 legislature passed a mental health bill. It created the position of commissioner of mental health and directed that a mental health program be developed. It included establishing training centers, an evaluation of all positions, provision of medical care within twenty-four hours of admission, creation of geriatric units, creation of a tuberculosis hospital unit and children's units and the provision of recreation, occupational therapy and vocational rehabilitation. These changes were to be implemented on June 1, 1949.[18]

The governor led a policy effort as well, which was reflected in a new law that recognized, "mental illness as a sickness with respect to which there should be not stigma or shame . . . and the necessity of adopting a program which will furnish dignity and hope for the patient, relief from anxiety, for the patient's relatives, and recognition for the psychiatric worker."[19]

On Halloween night in 1949, the governor went to Anoka State Hospital and helped burn a pile of restraints. The speech he gave on the occasion—perhaps the most notable event of the reform movement—is provided here.

STATEMENT BY GOVERNOR LUTHER W. YOUNGDAHL AT THE BURNING OF RESTRAINTS
Anoka State Hospital, October 31, 1949

It is just a little more than 260 years ago since mentally ill and other citizens were burned at the stake at Salem as witches.

A long period of time has elapsed since then. We discarded the stake but retained our attitudes toward the mentally ill, the voodooism, demonology, fears, and superstitions associated with witchcraft.

Tonight—Halloween eve—we employ the stake and fire for another purpose—to destroy the straight-jacket, shackles, and manacles which were our heritage from the Salem days.

As little as eighteen months ago all but one of our mental hospitals used mechanical restraints. Today most are restraint-free.

The bonfire which I am lighting tonight consists of 359 straight-jackets, 196 cuffs, 91 straps, and 25 canvas mittens.

No patient in the Anoka State Hospital is in restraint. These restraints were removed from the patients not by administrative coercion, but by the enlightened attitudes of the superintendent, staff, employees, and volunteer workers of the Anoka State Hospital. They were removed as the hospital's answer to witchcraft.

Governor Luther Youngdahl burning restraints at Anoka State Hospital, October 31, 1949. Courtesy Minnesota Historical Society.

> *By this action we say more than that we have liberated the patients from barbarous devices and the approach which these devices symbolized.*
>
> *By this action we say that we have liberated ourselves from witchcraft—that in taking off mechanical restrains from the patients, we are taking off intellectual restraints from ourselves.*
>
> *By this action we say to the patients that we understand them—that they need have no fears—that those around them are their friends.*
>
> *By this action we say to the patients that we will not rest until every possible thing is don't to help them get well and return to their families.*
>
> *We have no easy job. The roots of demonology are deep. We have burned one evidence of this tonight. We must be on our guard that it does not creep up in other forms—that what the bonfire symbolized tonight will carry on in public thinking until every last things is done to make the state hospital truly a house of hope for these most misunderstood of all human beings.*[20]

A picture of the event was covered in *Life* magazine along with an article that lauded the reform efforts in Minnesota, calling them the most heartening in the country. It stated that some patients at Anoka had been in restraints for twenty years prior to the reform.[21] The governor gave a series of radio talks as well, focused on garnering public support for continuing reforms.[22]

The commissioner noted that a distinction must be made between occupational therapy, vocational training and just plain work, saying, "It is insisted that this concept be accepted and adhered to so there is no possibility that slave labor is disguised as occupational therapy."[23] In the next two years, the number of occupational therapists in the state hospital system decreased from twenty-nine to three because non-professional workers were reassigned out of occupational therapy to become recreational workers or handicraft instructors, whose numbers went from zero to eighty-eight.

The increased funding produced many immediate improvements. At Anoka, neurosurgery could now be performed at the state hospital. Some psychotherapy was provided and a program was begun to review each patient's case and develop a treatment plan. This change signaled the shift from a custodial institution to a treatment center.

The use of restraints was eliminated except for rare cases such as postoperatively. Bed rails and sheet restraints were used for only two percent of bedridden cases. Chemical restraint use decreased to two and a half percent of the population. An occupational therapy research program began with the College of St. Catherine to discover the needs of patients. Sales for profit were discontinued. Emphasis was placed on rehabilitation rather than on mass production.

An art therapist and ten new recreational workers were added so seven wards were consistently served. A patients' orchestra was organized and movies shown six days a week. A softball team played a three-game series against Cambridge State Hospital. Evening entertainments increased, including bands, choral groups and variety shows.

The volunteer program expanded to more than 500. One recreational leader was assigned to liaison with volunteers, and a volunteer council was begun. A social service department was established and worked with an outpatient follow-up clinic in Minneapolis. The number of readmissions dropped to fourteen.

The number of patients per medical doctor dropped almost in half. Operating room and diagnostic equipment was obtained. Consultants were available once a week—twice as often as they had been. Payment was requested by families for glasses and dentures, but they were furnished even if no payment was received.

The number of employees at Anoka increased from 161 to 260. The work week was shortened to forty hours. The number of patients per employee per shift dropped from sixty-one to thirty-six. Patients now received the same food as employees, though prompt delivery continued to be challenging because of stairs and a lack of appropriate equipment. Some new kitchen equipment was installed.

Clothing was purchased and patients are allowed to choose what they wore. The seamstress was utilized for alterations. Brassieres, girdles, garter belts and men's garters were provided as needed. Men's dress shirts and suits were furnished to a limited extent. An adequate supply of sheets, pillow cases, blankets and bed spreads was provided. New, upholstered furniture for two day rooms was ordered and a radio placed in each ward.

Six cottages were redecorated. Front porches were rebuilt and sidewalks installed. The power plant was converted to AC. One building was remodeled into a tuberculosis unit. New water mains were laid and construction begun on three staff residences and a sixty-bed receiving hospital.

A three-week orientation program was provided for new aides. Physicians, the psychologist and social workers attended weekly presentations by Mayo Clinic staff.

The Anoka report ends with a quote from one of the volunteers:

> "We will never forget our visit to Cottage 2 when restraints were still used. We will never forget the distraught attitudes of these people—some badly disturbed, shouting, screaming, some having sunk into lifeless apathy born of lost hope. We still remember the patient wrapped up like a mummy who asked us if there was any hope for him in the new hospital program. We see some of these same people now folk and square dancing, conversing with volunteers and other patients. They are nicely dressed, and we think many look forward to getting well . . ."[24]

It is somewhat surprising, from that quote, that any volunteers came back after what must have been a horrific first experience. It's also illuminating to hear first-hand testimony that the *same patients* who had been restrained and were "badly disturbed, shouting and screaming" were able under different circumstances to participate in dances and casual conversation. This lends credibility to the view that it was the dysfunctional environment which produced much of the patient's disturbed behavior.

Improvements continued in other hospitals, as well. The use of tranquilizing drugs in Moose Lake decreased the use of shock therapy from ten percent of the patients down to one percent by 1958.[25] St. Peter stopped performing lobotomies during the 1957-1958 biennium.[26]

Fergus Falls, on the other hand, used its increased resources to intensify its use of electronic treatments during the next two years.[27] Cambridge began using shock therapy in 1960, whether for retarded or epileptic patients is unclear.[28]

Hastings unlocked all but the admitting and geriatric wards by 1960, and eighty-five percent of Moose Lake patients had ground privileges. Rochester had all but two wards open and Willmar had ninety-five percent open doors.[29] The incoming state medical director set an open door policy in July 1960. First Willmar, then Moose Lake, were one hundred percent open by the winter of 1962.[30]

NOTES

1. Willmar State Hospital, *Biennial Report*, June 30, 1938.
2. Willmar State Hospital, *Biennial Report*, June 30, 1943.
3. Minneapolis *Tribune*, May 24 2948 p. 5.
4. Public Welfare Department, Dr. Royal Gray, correspondence, 1950.
5. Minneapolis *Star*, Letter to the Editor, August 18, 1948.
6. Cambridge correspondence.
7. Grandquist, Luther. *Conscientious Objectors, Media Exposes, and Institutional Reform Brought Change for Many*. Access Press, May 10, 2010.
8. Unitarian Report.
9. St. Paul *Dispatch*, August 2, 1948.
10. Minneapolis *Tribune*, May 18, 1948, p. 10.
11. Minneapolis *Tribune*, May 24, 1948, p. 5.
12. Governor Youngdahl, speech on WCCO, May 5, 1948, Governor Youngdahl Records, speeches.
13. Cambridge correspondence .
14. Letter, Carl Jackson to Governor Youngdahl, November 19, 1948. Governor Youngdahl Records, Public Institutions.
15. Letter from Carl Jackson to Governor Youngdahl, November 19, 1948. Governor Youngdahl Records, Public Institutions.
16. Governor Youngdahl, speech to American Psychiatric Association, May 4, 1950. Governor Youngdahl Records, speeches.
17. Governor Youngdahl, speech on WCCO, May 5, 1948, Governor Youngdahl Records, speeches.
18. Office of the Commissioner of Mental Health, *The New Minnesota Mental Health Program*, 1950.
19. Governor Youngdahl speech to American Psychiatric Association, May 4, 1950. Governor Youngdahl Records, speeches.

20. Governor Youngdahl Records, Speeches.
21. *Life*, Nov 12, 1951, pp. 140-153.
22. Cambridge correspondence, Governor Youngdahl radio address, Nov 28, 1949.
23. *The New MN Mental Health Program*, Office of the Commissioner of Mental Health, 1950.
24. *Anoka Progress Report*, 1950.
25. *Welfare Report*, Fall-Winter 1958, p. 50.
26. *Ibid.*, p. 52.
27. *Welfare Report*, Fall-Winter 1960, p. 45.
28. *Ibid.*, p. 53.
29. *Welfare Report*, Fall-Winter 1956, pp. 45, 47, 48.
30. *Minnesota Welfare Report*, 1962, p. 24, 25.

CHAPTER NINETEEN
THE ERA OF PSYCHOTROPIC MEDICATION BEGINS

Most of the primitive and aggressive psychiatric treatments were eventually rejected in favor of psychotrophic medications and advanced talking therapies. Although medications eventually became the intervention that allowed thousands of patients to function in society, the early days of medication administration weren't always easy.

I remember their effect on one of my chronic patients. Her jaw constantly writhed and her tongue went in and out. She could talk and eat, but her appearance was startling. I was told that she had Tardive Dyskinesia, caused by a psychotrophic drug overdose many years earlier. Once the damage had been caused, it was irreversible.

Several of the old, aggressive treatments continued to be used on a limited basis. By the 1970s, ECT was still done several days a week at the Rochester State Hospital. I worked with a patient whose symptoms greatly improved, allowing her to be discharged after a series of ten ECT treatments. Nothing else had reduced her paranoia. I was surprised to discover that one of my mildly-retarded clients had received over 200 ECT treatments over the course of fifteen years. Did they contribute to her retardation? Although rare, one of my patients with severe obsessive-compulsive behaviors was given a lobotomy in the early 1970s. His family immediately took him home, so I couldn't gauge what it had done for him.

CHAPTER TWENTY
HOSPITAL CLOSINGS

THE PROCESS OF ENDING THE STATE HOSPITAL system began with what appeared, at the time, to be a relatively minor adjustment. A system was developed to keep patients closer to home and more connected to local services. A regional plan for mental health services began in 1961. Hospital receiving areas were aligned with community mental health centers. Regional mental health planning councils were established in seven regions of the state.

Each state hospital would be converted to a multipurpose regional facility serving the mentally ill, mentally retarded and chemically dependent. Implementing the new system involved transferring a number of patients back to their home region. Older patients were often discharged to nursing homes. St. Peter noted that the death rate among the long-term mentally ill who were transferred was much higher than those left in what had been their home for many years.[1]

Increased funding, lowered populations, and psychotrophic drugs led to many innovative improvements in patient care. Convalescent units were created in Fergus Falls in 1963-1964. Patients who could live independently, go to work every day, make their own decisions and work toward the better acceptance of themselves were selected for these units. Two wards had no nursing personnel at all, and the other only a minimum of nursing coverage.[2]

Anoka closed its farming program in May 1966, because its therapeutic value had almost disappeared with the advent of more modern treatments.[3] Other state hospitals' farm programs disappeared under the pressure to pay patients for working and the decreasing numbers of patients capable of working semi-independently.

A night-hospital program was begun in Anoka in 1965-1966. Patients spent the day in vocational rehabilitation facilities in Minneapolis, and returned to the hospital at night.[4] Fergus Falls utilized halfway houses on campus for patients who spent their day working in town.[5] Rochester developed a Comprehensive Mental Health Center program in 1966, which cooperated closely with local public and private agencies.[6] Finally, operant training was begun at Brainerd with severely retarded adults in 1968. These were described as historically forgotten and rejected patients.[7]

WELCH CONSENT DECREE

A LACK OF FUNDING AND CONTINUED overcrowding limited programming in facilities serving what were now termed retarded patients. The parent of a child in Cambridge initiated a lawsuit, in 1972, that would eventually bring an end to all state hospitals.

While much of the early focus of the lawsuit was on Cambridge, the Legal Aid Society of Minneapolis included residents of Faribault and Fergus Falls in a class action suit.[8] On February 14, 1974, the court found that civilly committed persons had a right to minimally adequate treatment. State officials were obliged to place plaintiffs in the least restrictive conditions feasible and improved staffing levels were specified.[9]

This was a radical departure from the view of the state's versus the individual's rights exemplified by the U.S. Supreme Court's decision in 1927.[10] The earlier ruling had given society the right to limit a person's reproductive rights, based on a perception of how much someone could contribute to society. Now, the court said that if the state confined a person to a hospital, that person had a right to treatment. It marked the end of the practice of eugenics in Minnesota state hospitals.

Governor Anderson said he agreed with the judge's orders, but didn't request additional funding, and the 1975 legislature didn't provide the funds necessary to comply with the judge's order. The judge, in 1976, ordered state administrators not to prevent the Commissioner of Public Welfare from hiring more staff, saying the state had treated the plaintiffs in an inhumane and unconstitutional manner.[11]

The state appealed this court interference, saying that determining staffing levels—and resulting expenditures—were a matter for the legislature and governor. Newly elected Governor Perpich told the District Court that he agreed with the goals in the court order, and would close Hastings and Anoka State Hospitals in order to free up more funding.[12]

The court gave Minnesota time to comply. The 1977 legislature responded by voting to close Hastings, but didn't allocate funds to increase staffing at Cambridge. Later that year, an agreement was reached to assign staffing positions freed up by the Hastings closure to Cambridge, and a court monitor was appointed to review compliance.[13]

That didn't satisfy parents, and in 1980, the agreement was expanded to include all state institutions housing mentally retarded patients. The population of the mentally retarded would be decreased by about 100 persons per year. Admissions could only occur if community placements weren't available, and counties had to develop community placements within a year for any child admitted to a state institution.[14]

Daytime activity center programs proliferated to serve retarded adults during the day. A free public education was federally mandated for children under twenty-one, beginning in 1974. Thus, schools and DACs provided individualized education and habilitation programs that served retarded clients during the day.

An early strategy to find residential placements and reduce state hospital populations was to place patients in nursing homes. These, however, proved to be inappropriate for many retarded individuals. The Department of Public Welfare developed Rule 34 in 1972, protecting the rights of retarded individuals to a normal living situation. A number of non-profit and for profit group homes began opening in Minnesota as residential facilities for mentally retarded children and adults. They provided smaller, more home-like settings, and evolved from mini-institutions to utilizing remodeled family homes.

In 1975, the legislature created an MR Family Subsidy Program. A Department of Public Welfare report five years later documented its success, saying, "The purpose was to give an alternative to placement of MR children outside their own homes."[15] By 1980, the program had been expanded to provide grants to 105 families. It reimbursed families for services they needed in order to keep their child at home. These could include transportation, equipment, home nursing and home health aides.

The report went on:

> It is assumed that a mentally retarded child will profit most
> from being reared in his own home. A side effect of a retarded
> child remaining in his own home is a decrease in family ten-
> sion and feelings of guilt about having a child living in a set-
> ting away from the family home. However, the other side of
> this is a possibility of exhaustion of family members, tensions,
> funneling of family money into meeting the needs of their
> retarded child to the detriment of other family members, lack
> of response to programs, or actual regression by the retarded
> child who reacts to the family tensions and exhaustion. If,
> with the input of funds to meet specific needs, the family
> problems can be decreased and the child's needs met, both
> the child and his family should benefit, hopefully to the point
> where the child can remain in his own indefinitely." [16]

The report concludes, "I do project that the MR Family Subsidy Program will prove to be of sufficient value that it will become a major Minnesota program for mentally retarded children and their families."[17]

The program came to be known as Waivered Services—meaning that
families accepted money for services needed to keep their child at home and
waived the opportunity to place their child in an institution.

State Hospitals Close

In the 1970s, declining populations in state hospitals led to discussions
in the legislature about closures. Closing Anoka was proposed, but Hastings—the smallest facility in the system—became the focus. For several
years, the state Senate voted to close it, while the House of Representatives
voted to keep it open. In 1977, Governor Perpich listed closing the hospital
as one of his priorities, in order to comply with a court order.

House members pushed to convert the facility to a state veteran's
home. The Senate wouldn't commit to creating a new veteran's home, but a

compromise committee agreed to close Hastings the following spring, with a million dollars set aside for future remodeling. All state hospital employees would be given the choice of transferring to other state employment or accepting up to $3,000.00 in severance pay. The 130 patients would be transferred to other facilities.[18] Hastings State Hospital closed on May 1, 1978, and the Hastings Veterans Home opened on the site three days later.[19]

State hospital populations continued to drop, and there were 1,000 empty beds in the system during the 1981 legislative session. The chemical dependency unit in Rochester State Hospital had been harshly criticized in a March report by the Department of Health. As a result, the director of the chemical dependency program was transferred. The report made Rochester a focus of criticism. Senate staff had developed a ranked list of possible state hospital units to close. First on the list was the expensive medical-surgical unit at Rochester, which provided services to the rest of the state hospital system. The chemical dependency and retarded units at Rochester were also high on the list because of recent criticisms.[20]

Republican Governor Al Quie called for reduced state spending. The DFL-controlled house and Senate each developed budget proposals. The House version included funding for Rochester, but was sixty-two million dollars higher than the Senate version, which called for closing Rochester.[21]

Wrapped in budget discussions, the Senate proposal to close Rochester State Hospital received little attention during hearings. When it came up before the full Senate, charges of political bias were raised. Of the nine state hospitals, only Rochester was represented by all Republican legislators.[22] Arguments at the capital became quite heated, and an outcry was raised from Rochester. Figures on how much might be saved were disputed on both sides. The closing was part of a larger Health and Human Services bill that included cuts to social programs the DFL had reluctantly agreed to.[23]

Governor Quie hoped that the hospital closing wouldn't make it out of a House-Senate conference committee. If it did, he would either have to sign it and accept the closing or veto the entire bill, opening the door to having to renegotiate other cuts.

Days before the end of the session, House members caved to political reality and accepted the hospital closing as part of reconciling the Health and Human Services Bill. The governor indicated that he wouldn't veto it. The surgical and chemical dependency units at Rochester would close within weeks, and the entire hospital would be closed in June of 1982.[24]

There had been no talk of alternate uses for the campus, except for the hope that several small non-profit groups would buy the buildings they had been leasing. Rochester business and civic leaders bemoaned projected economic losses. Staff had vociferously argued that the move was bad for patients. The debate had been acrimonious in the House and Senate.

The Department of Public Welfare prepared a report about the hospital closing processes six months after Rochester closed.[25] They found that the remaining state hospitals were operating near capacity, and the state hospitals continued to be the resource of last resort when there was no local money to pay for a patient's care.

Hastings had a relatively small staff of 199, was located close to the Twin Cities and offered employment at the new veteran's home. These factors allowed about half the staff to transfer to other state positions, while the remaining half received severance pay.[26]

Rochester had 538 employees, and only about 100 transferred to other state jobs. The rest took early retirement, were laid off or resigned with severance pay. The Department's preliminary figures showed personnel expenses in closing Rochester of two-point-seven million dollars, primarily in severance pay and unemployment. Their conclusion was, "In summary, cost savings resulting from closure of state hospitals do not result for, at least, several years—if ever."[27]

The Rochester State Hospital grounds and buildings were sold to Olmsted County for one dollar. The loss of the hospital was tempered when the federal government bought the buildings and about a third of the grounds in 1983, for a federal prison capable of providing skilled medical care.[28] No other state hospital would be abruptly closed without an announced alternative usage for at least part of the facility.

A thread running through the 1989 legislature was about getting tough on crime. They approved converting some of the buildings at Faribault and Moose Lake State Hospitals to medium-security prisons.[29, 30] Moose Lake closed as a state hospital in 1995. Some buildings at Faribault housed retarded patients until July 1998.

One of the first conversions the federal government did at Rochester, and which the state completed at Moose Lake and Faribault, was the construction of fences surrounding what were now prisons.[31] Society had never come up with the money to pay for fences to keep psychiatric patients in those same buildings safe, but immediately ponied up funds to keep the public safe from prisoners.

A new 200-bed facility was constructed on the grounds of Anoka State Hospital, to provide the Twin Cities with inpatient chemical dependency and short term psychiatric services. Patient populations at the remaining state hospitals continued to dwindle. Parts of the facilities were utilized for a number of new programs to serve each region. County social workers played primary roles in providing services to patients with mental illnesses and developmental disabilities.[32]

Many of the developmentally disabled went to small group homes. Programs were developed to allow families to keep children with disabilities at home. Patients with mental illnesses were placed in nursing homes, group homes, and supported apartments, and some were given allowances to find their own housing.[33]

Plans were initiated in 2002 to close what was then called the Willmar Regional Treatment center. The campus was purchased in 2006 by a conglomerate of companies.[34] After the initial uproar surrounding closing the first two hospitals, the system quietly shrank. There was no real end to this process, because small state-operated treatment facilities continue on the grounds of what were state hospitals.

Gillette

From its beginning, Gillette State Hospital was subject to the same economic stresses as the rest of the state system. At first, families had to supply clothing for their children, who stayed for up to two years. The Board of Visitors noted in 1910 that,

> At this institution the children are absolutely dependent for
> clothing on what is sent from their homes or supplied by

friends. And to a large degree, the homes of these children are typical of the poorest class of citizens. As a result, the children are not properly clothed. The difference between their scant apparel, and the nice warm suits and dresses of the children of the Owatonna State Public School, is most marked. We strongly urge that the legislature appropriate sufficient money for the State Board of Control to furnish the children of this state hospital with clothing the same as is humanely done for the children of the Owatonna Sate School.[35]

A major difference with the rest of the state hospitals was that children were not committed to the institution, so overcrowding didn't occur. Gillette's location near St. Paul and public sympathy for poor handicapped children resulted in a steady stream of publicity and volunteers.

In the 1930s, a few trauma cases were seen, but care emphasized orthopedic surgery and appliances. Infants were admitted for feeding problems

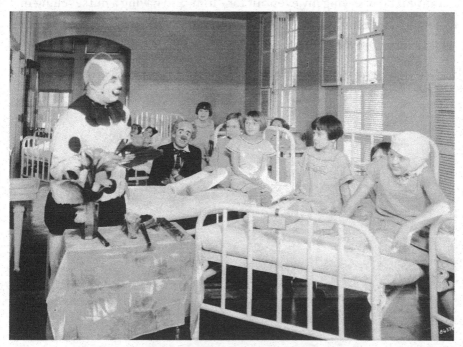

VFW circus entertainers, Gillette State Hospital ca. 1930, courtesy Minnesota Historical Society. Gillette enjoyed widespread support from civic groups.

for the first time, and a waiting list developed. Children with pulmonary tuberculosis weren't admitted. School was held from 9:00 a.m. until 4:00 p.m., with interruptions for dressing changes, physiotherapy and sun treatments. Nine teachers taught a population that averaged 200 patients. Religious instruction was provided weekly. It was felt that, "Character building is of as much importance to the child's future as correcting his deformity, and here both can be accomplished at the same time."[36]

The hospital included a swimming pool and library. A number of civic organizations donated money and services. Recreation activities included dances, singing, movie parties and band concerts. Patients were taken to the Ice Follies, circus, concerts and for an airplane ride. Boy Scout meetings included bedridden patients.[37]

But the hospital wasn't always so cheerful for patients. Patients recalled making beds with the blankets so tight they would bounce quarters, and lining up the beds in perfect rows. Nurses ripped up unsatisfactory beds and assigned the culprit to make younger boy's beds.[38] A man recalled, "I remember my first day, crying my eyes out for Mom, and having a nurse telling me to shut up and eat my supper; a parrot, falling down a window well, yelling, 'Help, Nurse, get me out of here.'"[39]

Boys' workshop, Gillette State Hospital ca. 1905, courtesy Minnesota Historical Society

On the other hand, a nurse remembered the time a ward supervisor and doctor violated the rules and allowed a two-year-old blind girl onto a ward with older girls. She had been in the hospital since infancy, and was thought to be retarded. She flourished in the enriched environment and quickly learned to talk. As an adult, she found work as a typist and got married.[40]

Changes in the private healthcare system and other state hospitals led to improved working conditions for staff. Nurses were granted a forty-four hour weekly work schedule in April 1948. Aides and other non-nurses signed a petition and sent it to the governor shortly afterward, asking for their schedules to be reduced from forty-eight to forty-four hours. Other state employees had already been given forty-hour weeks.[41]

The institution was renamed Gillette Children's Hospital in 1971. It became a public nonprofit organization in 1973, and two years later, was funded entirely by third-party payers. The old pavilions were abandoned in 1977, in favor of the modern hospital now in use. In 1989, Gillette became a private nonprofit organization, no longer under state control. The current name, Gillette Children's Specialty Healthcare, was adopted in 1996.

NOTES

1. Memo, St. Peter administrator to Friends of St. Peter State Hospital, March 19, 1973, security hospital scrapbooks.
2. *Minnesota Welfare Report*, Winter, 1964, p. 35.
3. *Minnesota Welfare Report*, Winter, 1966, p. 27.
4. *Ibid.*, p. 28.
5. *Ibid.*, p. 30.
6. *Ibid.*, 1966, p. 34.
7. *Minnesota Welfare Report*, Winter, 1968, p. 35.
8. *Rise Reporter*, November 2002, www.mnddc.org/past.
9. Welch v. Likins Memorandum; www.mnddc.org/past.
10. *War Against the Weak*, p. 121
11. Granquist L. *Minnesota: Budget balancing or a lack of due process?* www.access-press.org/2011.
12. *Ibid.*
13. *Ibid.*
14. Welsch v. Noot, Consent Decree, September 15, 1980, www.mnddc.org/past.
15. Shirley Bentson. MR Family Subsidy: Report July 1, 1980. www.mdddc.org/past.

16. *Ibid.*
17. *Ibid.*
18. *St. Paul Pioneer Press*, May 19, 1977, p. 17; May 20, p. 1; May 25, p. 1.
19. Minnesota Veterans Homes History, www.mvh.mn.us/history.
20. *RochesterPost-Bulletin*, May 14, 1981, p. 14.
21. *RochesterPost-Bulletin*, May 2, 1981, p. 1.
22. *RochesterPost-Bulletin*, May 16, 1981, p. 1.
23. *RochesterPost-Bulletin*, May 18, 1981, p. 1.
24. *Rochester Post-Bulletin*, May 15, 1981, pp. 1, 6
25. Department of Public Welfare, *A Report Prepared for the Honorable Albert H. Quie, Governor State of Minnesota*, November 1982.
26. *Ibid.*
27. Department of Public Welfare, *A Report Prepared for the Honorable Albert H. Quie, Governor State of Minnesota*, November 1982.
28. Federal Medical Center. volunteer.truist.com/Olmsted/org/1320611.
29. Facility Information, MN Correctional Facility—Faribault. www.doc.state.mn.us/facilities/faribault.
30. Facility Information, MN Correctioanl Facility—MCF—Willow River—Moose Lake. www.doc.state.mn.us/facilities/willowriver.
31. Personal observation by author.
32. The Evolution of State Operated Services, MN Department of Human Services.
33. Letter, William Lightburn, Security Hospital Scrapbooks, March 19, 1973.
34. The Evolution of State Operated Services, MN Department of Human Services.
35. *Second Biennial Report of the Minnesota State Board of Visitors for Public Institutions*, 1910, pp. 32, 33.
36. *Gillette State Hospital Biennial Report*, June 30, 1934.
37. *Ibid.*
38. Letter, December 15, 1976, Gillette miscellaneous records..
39. Letter, July 21, 1976, Gillette miscellaneous records.
40. Letter, October 9, 1976, Gillette miscellaneous records.
41. Letter, Carl Jackson to Governor Youngdahl. Governor Youngdahl Records, Public Institutions, May 10, 1948.

CHAPTER TWENTY-ONE
WHO WAS RESPONSIBLE?

IN THE CLOSING DAYS OF THE 2010 LEGISLATURE, a resolution was passed apologizing for the past care provided in state hospitals. Advocates had worked for thirteen years to get it passed. Opponents feared an apology would lead to lawsuits from former patients or their families. Others felt it would be a slap in the face to former employees of state hospitals.[1]

Following is the text of the resolution.

A RESOLUTION

Apologizing on behalf of citizens of the state to all persons with mental illness and developmental disabilities who have been wrongfully committed to state institutions.

WHEREAS, since the founding of the state hospitals, now called regional treatment centers, in 1866, tens of thousands of Minnesotans with mental illnesses and developmental and other disabilities have been removed from Minnesota communities and committed to live in state institutions, where many of these Minnesotans have died and been buried in unmarked graves or graves that bore only a number; and

WHEREAS, some residents of these state institutions were forced to labor without compensation;

WHEREAS, some residents of these state institutions were subjected to medical experiments and procedures without their consent, including the routine subjection of women inmates to involuntary sterilizations; and

WHEREAS, some residents of these state institutions were subjected to punitive shock treatments, frontal lobotomies, aversive treatments, and isolation; and

WHEREAS, thousands of children grew up in these state institutions learning none of the comforts, joys, and cultural norms that are learned in family life; and

WHEREAS, thousands of parents whose children required intensive care were forced to make painful decisions about whether to institutionalize their children or to provide all the care and education they required themselves, incurring in the process immeasurable financial, career, social and familial burdens; and

WHEREAS, parents of persons with developmental disabilities were sometimes advised to institutionalize their children, and to break their familial bonds by making them wards of the state irrespective of the family's and community's ability to support and nurture these children, and

WHEREAS, these fellow Minnesotans were portrayed by some as subhuman organisms, as deviant individuals to be feared by society, and as eternal children unaccountable for their behavior and incapable of speaking for themselves or shaping their own lives, which greatly diminished their fellow citizen's ability and willingness to accept them for their own unique qualities; and

WHEREAS, institutional care for persons with developmental disabilities has been scientifically demonstrated to be detrimental to people's basic development, including social development, development of self-determination, and the development of the basic skills of daily living; and

WHEREAS, many Minnesotans once viewed this institutional treatment as acceptable and subjected tens of thousands of citizens to it, but now recognize how wrong this treatment was; and

WHEREAS, Minnesota's state institutions are closing and, through this process, their history and the acknowledgement of our collective responsibility for it may be forgotten; and

WHEREAS, people who were relegated to state institutions and their families have never received a formal apology from the state; and

WHEREAS, the states of Virginia, Oregon, South Carolina, California, and North Carolina have apologized for similar actions towards people with disabilities in their own state;

NOW, THEREFORE,

BE IT RESOLVED by the Legislature of the State of Minnesota on behalf of the citizens of the state that the state apologize publicly to all persons with mental illness and developmental and other disabilities who have been wrongfully committed to state institutions, acknowledging that it regrets this history of institutionalization of persons with those disabilities, and that it commits itself in their memory to move steadfastly to help Minnesotans with those disabilities who in the future turn to the state for services to receive them in the least restrictive manner.

BE IT FURTHER RESOLVED that the Secretary of State of the State of Minnesota is directed to prepare an enrolled copy of this resolution and transmit it publicly to appropriate organizations of people with disabilities and to the news media.[2]

The governor signed the resolution but noted, "However, it is important to note this resolution also negatively paints with a very broad brush the actions of state employees who, in most cases, took actions based in good faith and the scientific understanding at that time."[3]

The difficulties I have with that statement are twofold. In their very earliest days, Minnesota state hospitals provided humane environments that allowed many patients to be discharged. However bizarre we feel their treatment rationales were—bed rest, lots of milk and work—they attempted to meet people's needs. That approach became impossible when hospital populations kept expanding, leading to overcrowding and low staff ratios. That's not an example of "scientific understanding at that time," but a reflection of a lack of funding.

Crowded conditions in Minnesota state hospitals led to the mindset that deterioration in psychiatric patients was inevitable, and that the primary task of the institutions was to maintain control of a largely unpredictable and potentially dangerous population with the limited money available. The system of unpaid patient labor or forced idleness enforced with restraints was the logical outcome. How else could they run the hospital for pennies a day?

It is true that the vast majority of hospital staff were simply doing the best they could under the circumstances. It is particularly tragic that the highly effective behavior program pioneered at Hastings in the late 1930s was ignored.

The second objection I have with the governor's statement is that it focuses attention on state employees whose actions were a reflection of the public's will. The commitment laws, prohibition against marrying defective people and sterilizing the unfit were approved by substantial legislative majorities, and stood for years. They were the official policy of the citizens of the state. On a personal level, people were so concerned about social stigma that they were willing to reject family members labeled as defective.

It is not the state government that should be apologizing to past state hospital patients, but the citizens—us. Granted, the government symbolizes the will of the people, and was the instrument of carrying out policies. It is disingenuous to blame "it" for doing what we wanted.

Those who believe I am condemning the doctors or staff working in the state hospitals have missed part of what I've tried to convey. The people I worked with in the state hospital were some of the most dedicated and professional I've ever seen. The patients/clients were our responsibility twenty-four hours a day, seven days a week. We took that responsibility seriously, and I worked harder there than I ever needed to anywhere else.

So, how should I feel about what happened to state hospital patients sixty years ago? When I began researching, it was clear to me that those terrible people back in time and over there did terrible things. It came as a shock to realize that Americans had supplied an intellectual patina to Hitler's genocidal philosophy.

In Minnesota, it must have been the work of a few elitists who were to blame. Looking at the list of those who supported eugenics however, it encompassed leaders in business, medicine, education and religion. Moreover, sterilization and commitment laws and the conditions in state hospitals were the direct responsibility of the legislature and state government. Regular reports from the hospitals to state agency heads detailed conditions.

The public was well aware of how functional many state hospital patients were. State Fair exhibits sold beautiful handwork from each state hospital. Patients performed on the radio, dance halls and in marching bands during local parades. So locking up competent people for life was a reflection of the public's will at that time, and the citizens of the state were terrible.

Eugenics had spread the belief in hidden "germ plasm" so thoroughly that families rejected spouses, children and siblings. Not only did they rarely visit, many preferred not to receive mail with a state hospital return address. The rejection continued after death, with families preferring not to receive their relative's body. Hospitals complied with the preference for privacy by burying patients with only their hospital number to mark the grave.

State Fair exhibits, undated, courtesy Minnesota Historical Society. Thousands of fair goers saw each year that patients who had been confined for life were capable of producing exquisite handiwork.

State Fair exhibits, undated, courtesy Minnesota Historical Society.

As a third generation Minnesotan, I have to recognize that it was my parents and grandparents who voted and paid taxes during that period of time. They weren't terrible people, so what am I to think?

The self-righteous anger that filled me when researching was so satisfying. Safe, too, for the blame and responsibility was over there, with them. I had no part in it. As long as it was their fault, there was no need for introspection or, heaven forbid, action on my part. Honesty forces me to see that it was the Minnesota society that created these conditions, a society I am part of.

I'm led to agree with Pogo that, "I have met the enemy, and it is us."

Notes

1. Minnesota House of Representatives, Public Information Services, 3/25/2010.
   http://www.house.leg.state.mn.us/sessionweekly
2. http://wdoc.house.leg.state.mn.us/leg/LS86/HF1680.1.pdf
3. Minnpost.com/stories/2010/06/03

CHAPTER TWENTY-TWO
WHAT LESSONS CAN
WE LEARN?

COMPASSION

THE MAJORITY IN AMERICA HAS REPEATEDLY been willing to allow the government to strip the rights from minorities to protect the well-being of the larger group. The history of Minnesota state hospitals shows that liberty, reproductive rights (the sanctity of their own bodies), and even lives were taken from those deemed unfit.

It seems that we are able to ignore the suffering of others, as long as they're unseen. Hidden behind the façades of imposing buildings, state officials were aware that appalling conditions existed. It was clear that locking people on the wards led to their deterioration, but hospitals felt they had few alternatives. It was just something that had always happened to the insane.

There were known alternatives to allowing people to live in rat-infested buildings contaminated with sewage. Maintenance and appropriate equipment would have kept them safe from electrocution and being burned by hot pipes. Adequate provision for known safety hazards would have prevented suicides and self-injuries and reduced the need for restraints.

The relationship between conditions at the hospitals and the legislature was clear from the beginning. The 1892 Trustee's Report included the following statement about the need for replacing one of the wings at Rochester:

> It is unsafe and dangerous in itself and constantly endangers the whole hospital. This old building is a fire-trap which may, at any time, cause a conflagration disastrous to the whole institution and the lives of the inmates. We have called attention to this in each biennial report for the last ten years. The Commissioners of Lunacy have inspected and

condemned it in most emphatic terms. The Board of Corrections and Charities have frequently called attention to it as dangerous and pointed out where the responsibility of its continuance rested. Both these boards and the Board of Trustees have asked the legislature to remedy it, and endeavored to show them their great responsibility in the matter.[1]

A young assistant superintendent placed the responsibility where it ultimately resided. He was quoted as saying, "When you, the public, decide that you want this place run like a hospital; when you decide you want it run humanely, just say the word. If you put up the money, we'll provide hospitals. We don't maintain these conditions of shameful neglect because we're sadists, but because the public won't foot the bill."[2]

It's impossible to sort out the contribution to hospital reform "modern" treatments brought. Would the legislature have been willing, in the late 1940s, to put so much money into the hospitals if there was no hope of people getting better and being released?

It's not clear either what role the revulsion generated by Hitler's extreme practices of eugenic principals played. Did that drive a repudiation of the need to protect society from defectives' progeny?

There are some heroes in this story. Catholics, guided by their beliefs in natural law and the sanctity of human life, opposed sterilization and provided an organized resistance to its expansion. Governor Luther Youngdahl welcomed an inspection by a critical outsider. That enabled the next set of heroes, the Unitarian Conference, to carry out their system-wide review. The Minneapolis *Tribune* devoted significant resources to visiting state hospitals and published an extensive set of articles. Governor Youngdahl remained very active in promoting reforms.

Once conditions were exposed and treatments provided hope, societies' attitudes changed. In the mid 1960s, state hospital farms closed. Discharges and the pressure to pay patients for their work combined to make them unfeasible. By the 1970s, state hospitals in Minnesota began to be closed.

HUMILITY

TWO FORMS OF HUMILITY COULD HAVE gone far to ameliorate the effects of medical interventions practiced upon the insane. Self-questioning would have provided opportunities for more objective observations. A sense of perspective in time may have limited causing irreversible damage.

Any criticism of early psychiatric treatments must be tempered by the reality those doctors faced. Many of their patients were extremely unhappy, dysfunctional and deteriorating. All medical staff could offer was sedation, which caused its own problems.

In the face of hopelessness, drastic measures appeared justified. Two Nobel Prizes in Medicine were awarded for interventions now viewed with distaste. Julius von Jauregg was awarded the prize in 1927, for injecting syphilitic patients with malarial blood. Moinz won it in 1949, for developing lobotomies. It demonstrates an arrogance on our part to think that current practices make us so much better than these men who won the accolades of their peers. Yet as we look back, we don't want to participate in treatments that ultimately prove to be dangerous and damaging.

One of the conditions that contributed to the continuation of dubious practices was the bias of the observers. They simply saw what they wanted to see. Interventions that caused brain damage—insulin comas and lobotomies—resulted in regressed behavior. Patients' reasoning, functioning and higher order thinking skills diminished. These were noted but dismissed because they were also happier and docile. They could be released from restraints and perhaps even cared for at home.

Measured in these terms, the treatments worked. That patients also lost their personalities and, some observers said, their souls, was acceptable. Yet the moment anti-psychotic medications became available, these outcomes were viewed differently. The use of insulin was discontinued and lobotomies became rare.

A modicum of medical humility was needed. Treatments were developed that gave doctors great power to make changes, but should they? Looking at the whole of a patient's life, would these interventions lead to independence, autonomy and self-actualization? Is it right for one person to take these possibilities from another?

Adding to our contemporary discomfort with these practices is their permanent nature. The damage caused by an insulin coma or lobotomy was irreversible.

There is an arrogance of the moment that affects most professions. We think we know so much more than those ignorant practitioners who went before us. Therefore, we are comfortable acting on what we know to be true. Somehow the fact that in a few years people will look askance at our pitiful efforts is ignored.

We often must act from our current knowledge. Doing our best is presumably better than doing nothing. Building the best sewing machine we can is entirely reasonable. We may be using the best reading curriculum available for first graders and look back with regret years later when we see how much better a subsequent system worked. For those particular students there is no going back, and they will spend the rest of their academic careers on the platform based on what they experienced in first grade.

The arrogance of the moment becomes most applicable to irreversible medical interventions. Could less intrusive (and perhaps less effective) treatments suffice until something better is developed?

There is also the question of whether to participate in a flawed system. Everyone, from the groundskeepers, to cooks, to ward staff and nurses, helped maintain a state hospital system that failed to meet patients' basic needs and violated their human rights. What was the staff's individual responsibility? How should they have responded?

I struggle with the ethics of my own career. I spent my life providing inadequate services because the institutions I was working in were underfunded. The harder I worked and the better I did, the more I enabled the institutions to remain underfunded. If none of us tried so hard the system may have collapsed, bringing attention and needed improvements.

So what should I have done? I loved my work and was good at it. I made significant contributions to the lives of my clients. Should I have walked away because I knew they were not getting the services they deserved? My ego said they would have been worse off because I was serving them well. Yet by staying, I was part of a system that shortchanged them.

The same issues faced state hospital staff in the bad old days. What would I have done if I was a nurse's aide? Could I have taken pride in feeding and toileting forty-plus patients in restraints? At what point would things around me have been so bad that my conscience wouldn't have allowed me to stay? Many people working in a human service field will be faced with the same questions at some point in their careers.

WISDOM

WOULD I HAVE BEEN WILLING TO DENY the basic rights of people labeled defective? When I consider the very public support of so many of society's leaders at that time, I'm sure I would have acquiesced. After all, the U.S. Supreme Court, a former president and vice president, the most successful businessmen, many prominent universities across the country, politicians and ministers were in support. Belief in these measures was so persuasive that some mentally ill patients asked to be sterilized[3] and even lobotomized.[4]

This was not a mean-spirited attempt to hurt anyone, but an effort to bring about a better world. One with less disease and misery. Who am I, an ignorant individual, to resist such persuasion?

Yet, I must. We look back in horror at the results of those well-meaning attempts. Thank goodness there were those, even if a tiny minority, who were willing to stand aside and say, "This isn't right." The clearest statement I'm aware of was printed in opposition to the Supreme Court decision that Carrie Buck, a feeble-minded young woman, could be sterilized without her consent. The *Catholic Daily Tribune* said that she "has rights which the state has not given her, but which she possesses by the very fact that she is a human person."[5]

The challenge for us is to know when to stand separate from what almost everyone else sees as the truth. How do we know when are we an obstructionist weirdo, or one of the few who sees clearly? Denying anyone's humanity denies everyone's. "The greatest good for the greatest number" also means "too bad for the rest." Conditions like those in the bad old days of the state hospitals result.

Modern medicine will never again engage in the widespread practice of unproven treatments with such devastating permanent side effects. The incorporation of the practice of ethics throughout the medical system prevents it.

Perhaps what we need is the widespread application of formal, professional ethics to most institutions. How would legislatures, schools, units of government or businesses operate if their major decisions had to pass an ethics sniff test?

NOTES

1. *Seventh Biennial Report of the Baord of Trustees and Officers of the Minnesota Hospitals for Insane,* July 31, 1892, p. 8.
2. Minneapolis *Tribune,* May 13 1948, p. 11.
3. Reed, Sheldon to Ernest Schrader. University of Minnesota archive, Dight Institute—Birthright, January 16, 1651.
4. *Mad in America,* p. 62.
5. *The Lobotomist,* p. 233.
6. *Preaching Eugenics,* p. 151.

CHAPTER TWENTY-THREE
CURRENT CARE OF PEOPLE WITH MENTAL DISABLITIES IN MINNESOTA

PEOPLE WITH SEVERE PERSISTENT mental illnesses in Minnesota are living within the mental health system, are in jail, or are living on their own terms—including being homeless.

MENTAL HEALTH SYSTEM

SERVICE PROVIDERS

A FIRST TIER OF MENTAL HEALTH TREATMENT exists for those Minnesotans who have insurance and can afford it. Inpatient facilities and clinics provide superb care. Individuals who have difficulty controlling their thoughts or emotions receive a variety of medical, behavioral and talking interventions. Patients fortunate enough to also have family and supportive friends have a chance of achieving productive, satisfying lives.

Serious mental dysfunction can lead to an individual alienating those around them. Stable employment becomes impossible. Alone and impoverished, these individuals are dependent on the services the state provides. They encounter a much different mental health system.

A second cycle of reform took place in Minnesota in 1995. Funds were made available for community-based services, and the state hospitals were systematically closed. Minnesota's State Operated Services (SOS) serve people with mental illness, developmental disabilities, chemical dependency and traumatic brain injury. Adult mental health services include seven community behavioral health hospitals, each with sixteen beds that provide short term inpatient services, and the 200-bed Anoka-Metro Regional Treatment Center. A number of current state programs are housed on former state hospital grounds. These include Anoka, Brainerd, Cambridge, Fergus Falls, Willmar, and St. Peter.

The Child and Adolescent Behavioral Health Services provide inpatient psychiatric treatment and foster home services. Adults and children with disabilities are housed in small residential facilities through Minnesota State Operated community services. The Minnesota Specialty Health System at Brainerd serves people with traumatic brain injuries. In Cambridge, the Minnesota Specialty Health System houses adults with developmental disabilities with a history of legal problems or who present safety problems to themselves or others.[1]

Concerns

Staff I interviewed from social service, corrections and emergency rooms expressed concerns not about the short term inpatient services that were being provided, but for what is not being done.

Individuals with mental illnesses who stay out of trouble live on the fringes of society. Supplemental Social Security from the federal government, and state-supplied Cash Assistance program provides them just over $800.00 a month. They can also receive food support. With these limited funds, they have to make the co-payments which Medical Assistance requires for medications and medical expenses.[2] Housing, clothing and transportation eat up the rest. It's not surprising that some patients choose not to fill prescriptions or continue to participate in treatment programs that include fees.

Many communities don't provide a place or support for a social network. Safe, clean,and affordable living environments are limited. Case management from a county social worker as well as vocational and day services aren't mandated and are subject to budget cuts. Few communities provide a place or support for social networking.

By one estimate, thirty percent of emergency room visits in Olmsted County alone are based in needs arising from mental health and chemical dependency issues. Dysfunctional living situations cause tremendous stress that manifests itself in physical symptoms. Unlike Medical Assistance, emergency room visits are free, including the transportation if an ambulance has been called. Individuals experiencing withdrawal from drugs or chemical addictions feel awful and show up looking for relief.[3]

Emergency rooms can hold people for up to seventy-two hours if they are a danger to themselves or others. While this level of need is relatively rare, corrections staff complain that patients receive such brief care in three days that they repeat problematic behavior when released. Hospitals typically lose money on inpatient psychiatric services, and limit the number of these beds. In one recent case, no beds were available anywhere in Minnesota for a suicidal patient.[4]

Several counties have initiated programs that identify individuals who repeatedly use emergency room services. A social worker is assigned a limited caseload of these clients, and regularly visits them to ensure that their needs are being met. Initial indications are that this program can save hundreds of thousands of dollars in emergency room costs.

INCARCERATION

NATIONALLY, IT'S BEEN ESTIMATED that prisons hold three times more people with mental illness than psychiatric hospitals.[5]

Minnesota prisons run by the state house relatively few people, only those who are considered to present the most danger to the public.[6] Most of those incarcerated are in the Community Corrections program, operated by the counties.

Some Minnesota counties have been able to train law enforcement officers on how to quickly evaluate and interact when they encounter people with mental illnesses. Some also have post-booking services to help determine how prisoners should be processed. Few counties have a pre-booking capacity to direct offenders to appropriate psychiatric services before they enter the justice system.[7]

Precipitating factors leading to incarceration include indigent patients' inability to pay for medication and a lack of publicly supported treatment options. Emergency rooms typically hold psychiatric patients for only a very short time. State-run community behavioral health hospitals have limited space.[8] Long term voluntary in- and outpatient facilities aren't available.

When an individual has acted in a way that is unacceptable, the police are typically called. Olmsted County, where I live, has a relatively large and affluent population. This is reflected in a modern correctional facility and a well-staffed and trained justice system.

A significant number of deputies and police officers have received Crisis Intervention Team (CIT) training. They are aware of the symptoms of mental illness and chemical dependency. They've learned active listening and verbal de-escalation skills so they can respond in ways that may help the offender regain their self-control. CIT-trained officers are aware of community resources, and may bring the person to an appropriate facility rather than to jail. If an individual has been involved in repeated minor incidents, the county has a mental health professional available to visit them at home and suggest services to prevent future occurrences.[9]

During the booking process at the police station, a mental health screening has been required by the state since 2009. If the individual has been taking medication, a nurse is called in to ensure that current medications continue. The nurse will contact the care provider or pharmacy as needed. A forensic social worker will call in a mental health provider who will complete an evaluation that day, if needed.

If the crime committed was minor and non-violent—for example, shoplifting food—the social worker will work with the attorneys and judge to find an alternative care facility in the community and divert the individual from jail. More violent crimes will involve a civil commitment process. If found to be a danger to themselves or others, they may be committed to the Anoka Metro Regional Treatment Center. After release from Anoka, they may be returned to jail or to a community placement under court conditions.

Thus, from the time the police first have contact with an offender, efforts are made at a number of steps in the process to keep them out jail. Despite this, current estimates are that thirty percent of the people incarcerated in Olmsted County have serious mental health issues, and an additional thirty percent are chemically dependent.[10]

Steps are taken to protect those who are vulnerable while they are in the Olmsted County Detention Center. They can be housed in smaller units where they can be more closely observed. Discharge planning is provided for inmates with significant mental health issues, including mental health care and housing.[11]

One of the memories I will always carry is an afternoon visit to a juvenile detention facility. Several of us escorted a church youth group on a "do gooder" visit. One young man stood out because he was so physically and socially awkward. My background of working in special education led me to think he either had a severe learning disability or Asperger's Syndrome. Either would have caused him to be socially unskilled and vulnerable. His arm was bandaged because the other inmates had set him on fire.

HOMELESSNESS

MENTAL ILLNESSES AND SUBSTANCE ABUSE are only two of many factors that contribute to homelessness. While the debate continues about the overarching causes of homelessness—a lack of affordable housing versus unemployment, versus adequately paying jobs—people remain on the street. One source utilized surveys conducted over sixteen years by the U.S. Conference of Mayors. The data, from 2000, indicated that twenty-two percent of the homeless were severely mentally ill.[12] That percentage translates to 200,000 people.[13] These figures do not include veterans or substance abusers—two groups who may benefit from treatment.

Closing state hospitals across the country from 1955 to 1985 reduced the number of beds available by about 400,000.[14] It should not be assumed that those same people are now on the street. Nevertheless, juxtaposing the former capacity of treatment beds with the number of homeless people currently needing treatment is sobering.

We might castigate the old state hospital system that saw TB rates that were only forty times the state average and accuse them of passive euthanasia. Clinical data on the homeless today finds current TB rates as high as 300 times the national average.[15]

Most Americans would agree that people who are mentally ill could be considered "worthy" of help. They didn't choose to be ill. The number and range of treatment facilities available to help them are inadequate. The primary barrier to providing adequate service remains what it was a hundred years ago—money.

Society hasn't yet come to grips with the issue of the right to refuse care. The solution will be neither clear nor simple. In other words, an eccentric individual who chooses to spend a Minnesota winter in a tent and has the skills to do so must have his rights respected (assuming he's not trespassing or violating health laws). The individual sleeping under a bush in the park who is confused and inadequately dressed, on the other hand, risks frostbite or death and should not be left there. A concerted effort by advocates, lawyers and lawmakers could develop a nuanced system that, when matched with adequate treatment and housing options, results in humane care.

CURRENT SERVICES FOR PEOPLE WITH
DEVELOPMENTAL DISABILITIES

THE LEGISLATURE PASSED A SERIES OF LAWS in 1975 that formed part of the Mental Retardation Protection Act. It struck down the old prohibition that defectives couldn't marry. Legal counsel was provided for individuals facing hearings on guardianship or commitment. Sterilizations and other treatments were permitted only when it was judged to be in the best interest of the client.[16]

By the 1980s, Minnesota had developed a four-part system that served retarded individuals and their families quite well. School and day activity programs provided individualized instruction and activities designed to increase skills in a caring environment. Individuals were housed in home-like settings, or their own homes.[17]

Costs expanded along with the programs. Special education for children was federally mandated and largely funded by local school districts. While some federal funds were available for day programming and residential services, much of the cost fell on counties and the state. Expanding costs could be contained by limiting how many residential facilities could be constructed, and by limiting the number of waivered service grants. Waiting lists developed both to get people into group homes, and for waivered services.

When the state budget was in good shape, new group homes were approved, and more waivered slots created. If there was a budget crunch, expansion would slow or stop. Given that additional people are born with disabilities each year, this created increasing waiting lists.

The lack of funding support for services to the developmentally disabled is particularly galling to me, having served children with disabilities in my professional life. Given that the life of a political promise can typically be measured with a stop watch, it is extremely naïve on my part to think back to the deal that was made with parents of retarded children back in the 1980s. In exchange for closing state hospital facilities for the retarded, group homes and day programs would be created, and families wishing to keep children in their own homes would be given adequate support. It seemed like such a wonderful alternative.[18]

I had worked in state facilities, where the only time residents got staff attention was when they misbehaved. As a result, some of them did misbehave—in spectacular fashion. Masonry walls and bare dayrooms minimized the possibility that an object would be eaten or thrown. One-to-one staff interaction with a resident was fleeting, at best. Everything was regulated by efficiency, and it was in no way a home or family environment.

As a school therapist, I witnessed family after family struggle to care for their child at home. The burdens were horrific. Impossible medical bills piled up, years would go by without an uninterrupted night's sleep, medical emergencies were terrifying and common, exhaustion was the norm and siblings were ignored. Unable to cope with the stress, parents came to resent each other because no one's needs were being met. These weren't marriages in any recognizable sense, but disaster zones. Divorces were the norm, and then usually the woman would be left to cope, alone.

The new systems would fix this, offering humane placements outside the home for families who couldn't keep up with twenty-four hour care demands. Other families could get the in-home services they needed to keep the household going. And then budget constraints hit, and the waiting list to get in-home help stretched from months, to years. If things got to be too much while waiting, there were no openings in group homes, leaving families where they had been before—left on their own.[19]

In the old days, the retarded were hidden behind the walls of large institutions. While not in the public eye, inspectors, reporters, advocates or parents could visit and create an uproar about deplorable conditions. The problems were the fault of the institution.

Now, families left to cope on their own are hidden from public view. One household at a time, behind closed doors, they struggle to accomplish the impossible. The entire burden is placed on the parents, who feel they are failures. They may not be able to completely carry out complex medical procedures or schedules. Perhaps they can't afford a service or piece of equipment that was recommended. Their healthy children are left to largely raise themselves, and perhaps give up much of their childhood to assist in caring for a sibling. Enriching, fun family activities are things that happen on other planets.

The worst aspect to me is the lack of public awareness. During legislative budget debates, a simple line item states that waivered service slots will be limited to "X" number. Perhaps an advocate group says the waiting list is "X" families long. What does that really mean? How much attention does that generate?

If a reporter wished to find out what was going on, they'd first be faced with privacy barriers. Who are these families? They're buried in the bureaucracy. Any family that was located would have to be willing to open its doors to let a stranger see that they were failing—in their own eyes—as parents.

These issues are not limited to children, either. Some parents dedicate their lives to caring for their disabled child, long after they've become an adult. Now the needs of the child and the abilities of the aging parent are no longer compatible and they need assistance.

What an ideal political arrangement. The needs of some of the most vulnerable people in our state are hidden away. Caregivers have sheltered society by keeping the burdens within their families. They often put icing on the cake by blaming themselves when things fall apart. What a wonderful way for the rest of us to save money and avoid responsibilities.

METO

THE TEMPTATION TO RESPOND HARSHLY to challenging behaviors in underfunded and potentially dangerous residential settings surfaced recently in several state facilities.

As Cambridge was closing down, a few of the buildings were retained for use by a statewide program. The Minnesota Extended Treatment Options, or METO, served up to forty-eight clients. Developmentally disabled adults who posed a risk to public safety were civilly committed. Residential, vocational and day program services were provided, as well as treatment for mental health, sexual abuse, substance abuse and those who committed criminal offenses.[20]

The Minnesota State Ombudsman for Mental Health and Developmental Disabilities investigated a complaint about the use of restraints at METO. The ombudsman's office issued a report in September 2008, highly critical of the use of restraints at METO. They found that sixty-three percent of the residents had been restrained, some as many as 299 times in a year. Regulations limiting restraint periods to fifty minutes were ignored. Devices used included restraint boards, handcuffs, leg hobbles and posey cuffs.[21]

Rather than using restraints as a last resort when faced with imminent risk to the patient or others, residents often calmly complied with directions to assume positions so restraints could be applied. Thus, restraints were used not as a safety measure, but a punishment. Once the restraints were applied, residents became uncomfortable and began crying, yelling and struggling. Since METO policy stated that the person had to have been calm for fifteen minutes before the restraints could be removed, this lengthened restraint periods.

The Department of Health also investigated, and issued a memorandum finding that METO also used chemical restraints on residents, including Haldol, Ativan, intramuscular Benadryl and Zyprexa. The Department of Human Services issued a corrective order, citing numerous violations of state laws.[22]

These findings were used to request an injunction filed in July 2009, by parents of several residents. The parties negotiated a settlement agreement that resulted in closing METO. The state agreed to provide residents with safe and humane living environments free from abuse and neglect.[23]

The Specialty Health System was created, providing person-centered planning, positive behavioral supports and family feedback. Restraints could not be used as punishment. Individuals at St. Peter Security Hospital and

Anoka Metro Regional Treatment Center committed solely with a development disability would be transferred to an integrated setting.[24]

ST. PETER SECURITY HOSPITAL

THERE WERE SUBSTANTIATED REPORTS OF patient abuse at St. Peter Security Hospital in 2011. Restraints were used 225 times and patients spent 1,772 hours in seclusion. Employees were seriously injured nienty-seven times, two-thirds occurring from patient assaults. Patients suffered 310 injuries— only twenty percent of which were caused by patient on patient assaults. Many injuries occurred when employees tried to restrain or confine agitated patients.[25]

The Human Services Commissioner hired a new administrator who mandated a policy of minimal restraint and seclusion. Most of the psychiatrists at the hospital accused him of a combative and difficult management style, and resigned. As this is written, the treatment staff hasn't been rebuilt.[26]

NOTES

1. www.dhs.state.mn.us 10/2011.
2. Phone interview, Olmsted County social worker, April 2012.
3. Interview, emergency room physician, April 2012.
4. Interview, emergency room physician, April 2012.
5. William Kanapaux, "Guilty of Mental Illness," *Psychiatric Times*, Jan 1, 2004.
6. Phone interview, MN Department of Corrections spokesperson, October 2012.
7. Phone interview, Olmsted County social worker, April 2012.
8. *Post-Bulletin*, Dec 5, 2009, p. B5.
9. Phone interview, Olmsted County social worker, April 2012.
10. Olmsted County corrections staff.
11. *Ibid.*
12. U.S. Conference of Mayors, cited in Wright, Kelly, *Homeless in America*, Gale Group, Detroit, 2002 p. 14.
13. Roleff, Tamara. *The Homeless*, Greenhaven Press, San Diego, 1996, p. 177.
14. Baum & Burnes, *A Nation in Denial*, Westveiw Press, Bounder, 1993, p. 163.
15. *Homeless In America*, p. 73.
16. MN Statutes 1976, 252A.01. www.revisor.mn.gov.
17. *MR Family Subsidy: Report July 1, 1980*. www.mnddc.org/past.
18. *Ibid.*
19. www.projusticemn.org/session_summaries.

20. "Minnesota Extended Treatment Options," www.minnesotahelp.info/public 12/2/2011.
21. Case 0:09-cv-01775-DWF-FLN, Filed 07/19/10, United States District Court, District of Minnesota. www.clearinghouse.net.
22. *Ibid.*
23. "Brief Summary of Key Points," Minnesota Governor's Council on Developmental Disabilities, July 27, 2011.
24. *Ibid.*
25. Minnesota.publicradio.org/display/web/2012/02/28.
26. www. Startribune.com/politics/statelocal, February 9, 2012.

Chapter Twenty-Four
Personal Lessons
Learned

Spending years sifting through box after box of faded state hospital records became transformative for me. In a slowly building, at first unnoticed process, I became radicalized. The surprises kept coming, day after day. I discovered that sheriffs were allowed to grab people from anywhere, and committed people were usually only released to a family member. And then there were what I came to call "the outrage of the day:" finding proof of repeatedly lobotomizing a retarded teenager, carrying out a sterilization on a pregnant patient, sterilizing unmarried mothers, using IQ tests that falsely labeled people.

I tried to maintain a balanced perspective, and develop an understanding of why things were done. But these were not just abstract entries in a dusty ledger. I had worked with patients who lived through some of these events. I was immersed in misery, seeking understanding.

I came to conclude that it all comes down to one of the most fundamental questions—why are we on this earth? If it is to gain as much, personally, as we can—accomplishments, money, possessions or fame—then the state hospital history makes sense. We judge others by their usefulness. The more they can contribute to the wellbeing of myself and others, the more valuable they are. If their existence won't help me, they aren't important. If they in some way imperil my well-being, they are a menace. So if you're incapable because of a cognitive disability, you should be dealt with in the most economical way possible and you certainly shouldn't be allowed to reproduce. And that's exactly what the state hospitals in Minnesota did.

On the other end of the spectrum—which is where my studies moved me—is the belief that we are placed on this earth to provide an opportunity to become our best selves. Much of our daily efforts are to be expended in helping others. People are valuable simply because they exist. People can arrive at this conclusion from perspectives of philosophy, ethics, religion or spirituality (which is where I'm coming from). When viewing the lives of people with cognitive disabilities, the question changes from "What is most expedient for society?" to "How can we most fully enhance this person's life?" The answers must begin not with their disabilities, but with their priorities, goals and dreams. How can needs be met in a way that enriches this person's life—as they envision it?

Many would say this is a ridiculous, impossible approach. And under today's mental health system, it is. Excellent inpatient facilities exist to assist people who are causing problems for themselves, their families or communities. Once they're discharged, however, a common measure of success is that they're no longer creating difficulties. Unless they've committed a crime, we respect the rights of people with mental disabilities. We also often leave them to lead lives of social isolation and abject poverty.

Any major change in the care of people with mental illnesses or developmental disabilities would require a massive effort. We need research to develop a broad spectrum of medical, behavioral, social and habilitation interventions. What would it take to convince a homeless person to adopt a safer, healthier lifestyle? Safe housing? A supportive social environment?

Along with the research and program development, individualizing approaches would require far more money than is currently available. And that's where the problem lies—where it has always been. There is no doubt that if the state of Minnesota were to make an additional one billion dollars available for improved service to people with mental disabilities, lives would be dramatically improved. Doctors, psychologists, social workers and therapists would be thrilled at the opportunity to do things better.

Will we?

Chapter Twenty-Five
Conclusion

THE FIRST MINNESOTA STATE HOSPITAL opened at St. Peter in 1866. Two of the first patients were transferred from jail in St. Paul. One was a man who had been incarcerated for three years, the second a women who'd spent ten months in jail and arrived "perfectly covered with lice."[1]

We have in some ways come full circle, once again jailing those whose mental illness contributes to objectionable behavior. By leaving others homeless, we have regressed to the pre-asylum philosophy of casting people out. Just as it was in at the beginning of the twentieth century, the biggest obstacles to humane treatment of those with mental illnesses are inadequate funding and public indifference.

How will people a hundred years from now judge the way we currently treat those with mental illnesses? Will what we are now doing engender the same revulsion toward our current society that we feel when looking back at the bad old days in state hospitals?

With the exception of isolated cases of abuse, there is no indication that staff set out to produce misery. The severe lack of resources caused them to make decisions that routinely resulted in frustration, deterioration and death.

What would it have been like to be a patient in the bad old days? Labeled defective and facing a life sentence, you'd have to find your way in this strange place.

I'm quite certain that I wouldn't have the determination to demand to go home every chance I got, even after a lobotomy. I doubt that if I lost all my speech except for a single phrase it wouldn't display the defiance of, "Never will." Or that I could come up with a way to safely insult staff by asking them if they're a single or a double, privately adding the "shit" I felt should end the question. How many of us could maintain our anger to keep symbolically flushing our abusive brother down the toilet for fifty years, despite losing all our teeth and control of our facial muscles?

My patients did all these things. How am I to view them? As defectives? Leading weak, shattered, meaningless lives? Or as examples of amazing courage, resilience, determination and heart in the face of inhuman conditions? I prefer to feel that I was fortunate to witness the possibilities of the human spirit, albeit wrapped in tragedy.

NOTE

1. W. Erickson, MD. *The Great Charity: Minnesota's First Mental Hospital at St. Peter*, St. Peter Regional Treatment Center, 1991, p. 43.

APPENDIX
HOSPITAL FOR THE INSANE AT ST. PETER, 1960

THE FOLLOWING MAP IS PROVIDED not to identify individual buildings—the scale is too small. The security hospital was located near the Minnesota River, and enclosed by a fence. The main hospital building was in the center of the complex.

The campus sprawled across many acres, and included an incredible number of agricultural and industrial facilities. Note the railroad spur that curled around the back of the central building to deliver coal to the heating and power plant. The main rail line and river were adjacent to campus, and weren't fenced off.

Many of the buildings on this map have since been torn down.

LIST OF BUILDINGS

Administration Building	Storage
Women's Ward	Granary
Men's Ward	Greenhouse
Men's Ward	Wagon Shed
Detention Hospital	Greenhouse
Dormitory #1	Calving Barn
Print Shop	Cow Barn
Carpenters Shop	Calves
Cottage for Men	Hog Shed
Dormitory #2	Machine Shed
Offices	Corn Crib
Machine Shop	Garage
Women's Ward	Shoe/Tailor/Mattress Shop
Women's Cottage	Root Cellar

Hospital	Slaughterhouse
Nurses Home	Geriatric Building
Criminal Detention	Geriatric Building
Pump House	Hospital
Assist Engineer's Cottage	Service Building
Engineer's Cottage	Quarters
Blacksmith Shop	Superintendent
Granary	Power Plant
Laundry	Steward's Office
Fire House	Feed Mill

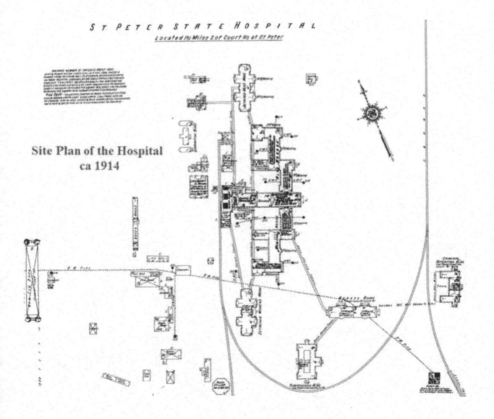

Site Plan of the Hospital
ca 1914

INDEX

211